Affirmative Exclusion

JEAN-LOUP AMSELLE

Affirmative Exclusion

Cultural Pluralism
and the Rule of Custom
in France

translated from the French by
Jane Marie Todd

CORNELL UNIVERSITY PRESS
ITHACA AND LONDON

Originally published by Aubier 1996, Flammarion 2001 for the preface, under the title *Vers un multiculturalisme français: L'empire de la coutume.*

The publisher gratefully acknowledges the assistance of the French Ministry of Culture–Centre national du livre.

First published 2003 by Cornell University Press
First printing, Cornell Paperbacks, 2003

Printed in the United States of America

Library of Congress Cataloging-in-Publication Data
Amselle, Jean-Loup.
 [Vers un multiculturalisme français. English]
 Affirmative exclusion : cultural pluralism and the rule of custom in France / Jean-Loup Amselle ; translated from the French by Jane Marie Todd.
  p. cm.
Includes bibliographical references and index.
 ISBN 0-8014-3946-9 (alk. paper) — ISBN 0-8014-8747-1 (pbk. : alk. paper)
 1. France—Ethnic relations—History. 2. Multiculturalism—France. 3. Decolonization—Social aspects—France. 4. Minorities—Cultural assimilation—France. 5. Muslims—France. I. Title.
 DC34 .A5713 2003
 305.8'00944—dc21   2002153020

Cornell University Press strives to use environmentally responsible suppliers and materials to the fullest extent possible in the publishing of its books. Such materials include vegetable-based, low-VOC inks and acid-free papers that are recycled, totally chlorine-free, or partly composed of nonwood fibers. For further information, visit our website at www.cornellpress.cornell.edu.

Cloth printing   10 9 8 7 6 5 4 3 2 1

Paperback printing   10 9 8 7 6 5 4 3 2 1

For Simon and Mathias

Until that time, therefore, French civil laws were not applicable to the Algerian natives; they continued to live as they always had, under the rule of their traditional practices.

—Léon Dunoyer, *Etude sur le conflit des lois spécial à l'Algérie,* 1888

Contents

Preface to the Second Edition

There is a contradiction at the root of the French Republic, between natural law and the rights of man on one hand and the management of cultural differences on the other. Natural law, as it was defined by political philosophy—and by Jean-Jacques Rousseau in particular—and the rights of man, as they were propagated by the French Revolution, seem at first glance incompatible with French multiculturalism as it was applied some time ago in the colonies and as it has continued to function in creating and dealing with the communities currently living on national territory.

The very existence of a specifically French anthropology is directly connected to that question. As the promised land of republican assimilation and the nation of the rights of man, France ought not to possess an anthropological tradition, that is, a science devoted to the recognition of ethnic and cultural differences. The principle of republican integration dictates that foreigners and colonized peoples are, over time, supposed to become full-fledged citizens. Even if that integration rests on a fiction, there is no category under which to classify these entities, which form the blind spot of the system. It is within that gray zone that the status of the "native" can be situated, a concept governing the hybrid categories of the French colonial empire.

It appears, therefore, that there is another principle underlying the operation of the Republic and that this principle is not so different from the way French sociologists, Emile Durkheim in particular, defined their political and scientific program. In order for republican integration to be achieved, a fusion of the different groups living on national territory had to come about. The republican model is thus viable only if it rests on the prior existence of a plurality of groups that, within the context of organic solidarity, are supposed to form a harmonious synthesis. That holist presupposition, which contradicts the methodological individualism implicit in the French doctrine of assimilation, was particularly apparent in the French colonial enterprises that occurred subsequent to the Enlightenment.

Unlike colonization under the ancien régime, which was based on mercantilism—primarily the slave trade—and on the conversion or redemption of colonized peoples, the later colonial enterprises operated chiefly on the principle of "regeneration,"[1] that is, on the advancement of the common people and the elimination of the despotic upper stratum. If the principle of regeneration was to function, it had to posit the existence of the old schema of war between the two races, whose genealogy has been carefully traced by Michel Foucault.[2]

The Liberal Communitarian State, or Affirmative Exclusion

That model of regeneration is currently being reactivated under the banner of the North American concept of multiculturalism. North American ideas have penetrated French society so thoroughly that French sociologists with very different theoretical positions all enthusiastically hail the virtues of affirmative action and multiculturalism, all the while forgetting the U.S. desegregation policies set in place in the 1960s, particularly in the schools (busing, for example). Thus Pierre Bourdieu, in one of his recent books, argues vehemently against egalitarianism and universalism, which he finds at fault because they are representative of what he terms "scholastic reason"; at the same time, he is careful to criticize relativism in a similar manner.[3] And Alain Touraine, in one of his recent books,[4] accuses the French state of homogenizing French society, even though that state has actually torn apart the social fabric to produce myriad communities. As a result, the notion of multicultural society that Touraine proposes is largely utopian, since it assumes that the subject forges an identity for itself stripped of any notion of community in order to communicate with other cultures, even as the state favors the solidification of communities.

Within the context of the privatization policies pursued for more than a decade, a play of mirrors is taking place between the welfare state, which increasingly seeks to unburden itself of its responsibilities, and nascent communities, which use the state's new role to demand their rights. But, contrary to all expectations, the French state, in becoming increasingly liberal (laissez-faire), encourages not so much individualism as the expansion of a "civil society" called upon to manage itself through a variety of organizations responsible for providing the various kinds of assistance once offered by the state.[5] We are therefore witnessing a mutual reinforcement of the liberal state and of the different communities, which has had the effect of relegating to the background the atomistic or egalitarian notions that have until now been the underlying principles of assimilation and full participation in the French nation. This development serves as a response to the concerns of Alexis de Tocqueville, who maintained that equality worked against freedom and believed that associations were the only means to counter the despotism inherent in the operations of democratic societies.[6] For those who champion an end to the welfare state, the time of republican egalitarianism is past; and a principle of equity, the only thing capable of protecting outcasts from the exorbitant privileges of those who have jobs, especially when those jobs are protected, ought to take its place.[7] For proponents of the liberal communitarian state, the abnormally high unemployment rate our country is experiencing is connected to the considerable social costs of government programs and social protection. If that were true, to set things aright after the collapse of communism, we would have to eliminate all traces of socialism from our economy.

In that event, what I call "affirmative exclusion" would have the responsibility of compensating for the dysfunction in our social system. The essential feature of affirmative exclusion, whether on the right or on the left, is to divide up national territory into a certain number of sectors or zones where the new management of the social factor can be applied. Like the World Bank, which strives to direct its operations toward "target groups" in the Third World, the supporters of French-style affirmative action are inclined to grant certain cities or neighborhoods privileged treatment by setting them up as "free zones" or "priority education zones"[8] or by establishing immigration quotas.

At the root of this policy is the idea that universalistic principles have failed and that the welfare state no longer has any power over the social realm. Special opportunities must therefore be given to the disabled of every sort, but without any possibility for society's losers to leave their exclusionary zone. In that way, a ghetto is created by regenerating pockets of poverty and disability. In reality, the tough neighborhoods ought to be opened and the residents allowed to mingle with the rest of society.[9] In addition, an extremely insidious social apparatus, based on the insurance model, has been set in place. It divides individuals between good and bad risks, life's winners and losers, and thus assigns every social actor to a "class" of privilege or disability. The result is a very close network that, far from producing discrete individuals in keeping with a republican principle or classifying them by social class in the socioeconomic sense of the term, endows each person with a specific weight depending on his or her place in a real or virtual group (deaf mutes, paraplegics, etc.). The result of this proliferation of identities is that individuals can no longer be compared to one another on an equal basis and that they lose personal responsibility for themselves. It is because of that unprecedented set of circumstances that the question of establishing a new social contract arises—a contract no longer among individuals, as in political philosophy, but among communities. At the ethnic and cultural level, two major institutions are set in place, the French nation on one hand, composed of those "of French stock," which can thus be assimilated to an ethnic group or race, and on the other, the different ethnic minorities or communities, which serve as a foil to French identity.[10]

The recognition of a multiplicity of ethnic groups in France thus offers ideal conditions for the rise of racism. The two different faces of the French state—a liberal state but also a communitarian racist state—can be seen clearly in the way the state has honored the commitments of the Vichy regime and in the genealogical search for racial purity as practiced by Sécurité Sociale, for example, which conducts surveys of French nationals born abroad. That is why the defense of the republican character of the French state, which some people consider obsolete, is indispensable if we wish to avoid the rise of jus sanguinis and the proliferation of differential treatment. The republican model, despite all its defects—which are linked in great part to its underlying polygenism—offers the only response to the segmentation of the population as it has been propagated and imposed by the French state. Rather than a French-style multiculturalism, we must move toward a multitude of private allegiances within the anonymous framework of French citizenship. As Jürgen Habermas, the author of *The Theory of Communicative Action*, has shown, a society cannot be reduced to a conglomerate of communities where an individual's freedom is linked to that of everyone else in a purely negative manner. As he argues, "on the contrary, the correct demarcations are the result of self-legislation practiced in common in such a way that, in an association of free and equal persons, all must be able to understand one another as the co-authors of the laws to whom they feel individually connected as their addressees."[11]

The Ambiguities of *Métissage*

Largely influenced by North American ideas, the liberal communitarian state—unlike its predecessor under Marshal Philippe Pétain in that respect—provides a structure receptive to multiculturalism, which it is now considered good form to declare the antidote to the inadequacies of the republican model of assimilation. Let us note, however, that this multiculturalist project is itself dependent on the instability of the republican model, which rests on the implicit schema of the war between the two races.

The defenders of multiculturalism, however well-intentioned, are not aware that their position, which consists of promoting the *métissage* (mixing) of the French population, amounts to defending a polygenistic notion of human settlement.[12] Although the obsession with the French nation's purity, as it is expressed by leaders in the National Front, for example, represents a racist position par excellence, the defense of *métissage*, as it is proposed by the supporters of multiculturalism, attests to the very same attitude, in that it presupposes an original separation that ought to come to an end.

Through multiculturalism, what is being expressed is the right to difference, in the sense that this ascribed difference goes hand in hand with the recognition of the other as other, that is, as a problem. It is therefore clear that the theme of multiculturalism or of *métissage* is connected to globalization.[13] At the human and anthropological level, globalization means nothing more than a return in force of polygenism. In answer to a past separation, which is believed to produce anxiety, globalization may appear to be the means to reconnect scattered segments. Economic globalization thus stands as the equivalent of the universal mingling of different human races (black, white, yellow).

The World Mix

In the face of this return in force of polygenism in the form of globalization, *métissage,* or "Creolization," it is urgent to return to the age-old debate that has troubled natural history and the natural sciences as well as their direct heirs, biology and genetics. The question of race is obviously at the heart of this debate. Physical anthropology and biology, having long grounded their discourse on the existence of race or of races, abandoned the paradigm of a variety of different human races and initiated a discourse that denies the existence of these same races. But parallel to that noble discourse regarding the nonexistence of human races, a discourse that is supposed to effectively counter the National Front version of the racism of purity, biologists, through genetics, are unwittingly introducing a new sort of racism, based this time on bloodlines. The research currently conducted on hereditary illnesses and on the human genome contribute toward reinforcing an idea profoundly rooted in the public's mind, which is related to Wittgenstein's "family resemblances." From that perspective, that modern geneticism would serve to support the innate belief that families inherit, not so much acquired traits as in Lamarkianism, as traits of the descent group as a whole (Weismann).[14]

In that sense, the problem of race is far from moot; and it is possible to predict, with little risk of error, that it will be at the center of discussions in the coming years. That is why the theme of *métissage,* which seems to be the antidote to that problem, is actually nothing but a symmetrical and inverted form of it. As animal husbandry demonstrates, one can only crossbreed entities that already exist as such, that is, distinct bloodlines. Only the intellectual—and not biological—postulate that there is a common humanity whose different segments have done nothing but continually mingle can counter the underlying racialism of the theory of *métissage.* But our current difficulty is in great part the result of our incapacity to conceive of cultural phenomena in anything but biological terms.

The world mix is a given in the constitution and continuation of our familiar environment, which cannot be assimilated to a patrimony—yet another form of bloodline racism—or to an inheritance of any kind. We must abandon the language of medicine and biology if we wish to conceive of *métissage* as it exists today, and we must turn instead to literary or philosophical metaphors. The model of a zero-sum homeostatic world seems to provide a useful toolbox for analyzing multiculturalism in that it allows us to avoid anxiety about both cultural decay and about the neutralization of cultural difference under the impact of *métissage*. Since the origin of time, world cultures have continually mingled. Hence the stitches being added today are sewn onto already "mended" products, the result of an earlier patchwork, and not on original segments of primordial cultures. They are, in some sense, a patchwork of a patchwork.

Affirmative Exclusion

Introduction

The idea of the French Republic, founded on the principle of the assimilation of citizens as individuals, appears contradictory to the concept of an initial opposition between two groups, the Franks and the Gallo-Romans, which has been central to a great deal of French historiography. Nevertheless, that oppositional schema lies at the heart of French multiculturalism, which, in its most recent and most extreme versions, culminates in the division of the population into minority "communities" on one hand and the majority "French ethnic group" on the other. It is within that context that we need to situate the hardening of identities and the rise of ethnic and religious fundamentalism that are affecting France.[1]

I am, of course, not the first to wonder about the compatibility between republican universalism and the founding schema of the history of France—namely, the war between the Frankish and the Gallo-Roman races. The historian of ideas Léon Poliakov, among others, has expressed astonishment at the coexistence of these two principles and sees them as one of the possible causes for the recurrence of heated struggles in France and the particularly intense nature of social confrontations in that country.[2] It is perhaps no accident that this schema is resurfacing at the very moment when integration seems to be becoming problematic, and when the foundations of the Republic seem to be once more called into question.[3]

It is as an anthropologist specializing in sub-Saharan Africa, and not as a historian of ideas, that I would like to examine the preeminence of the schema of the "war between the races," both within the context of national history and in terms of the exportation of that schema to the colonies. In fact, the history of the metropolis and that of the colonies, far from constituting two hermetic spheres, have continually influenced each other, to such an extent that the treatment of minority communities within the borders of France borrows a great deal from colonial precedents.

The "War between the Races"

French national character passed through several phases in its genealogy, which I would like to mention briefly before evaluating the current impact of that character. Simplifying grossly, let us note that, from an anthropological and raciological perspective, the history of France has oscillated between unity and multiplicity, though we need to distinguish between different notions of unity, and in particular, between what we might call "original unity" versus "fusional unity."

By "original unity," I mean the hypothesis that the two major populations residing on our soil—the Franks and the Gallo-Romans—had a common origin. Seventh-century scholars, in postulating that these groups both came from Troy, wanted to maintain the cohesion of the nation and to reinforce the ties both with Greco-Roman antiquity and with the Old Testament. It was with the Renaissance that this thesis of an origin common to the Franks and the Gallo-Romans was discredited and a dual origin substituted for it: the Franks, ancestors of the nobility, were considered Germanic; the Gallo-Romans, ancestors of the common people, had an autochthonous origin. That interpretation was particularly influential in that it was adopted by

2

several different camps: by the aristocrats with Henri de Boulainvilliers, by the monarchists with Jean-Baptiste Dubos, and
by the republicans with Gabriel Mably. Despite all the differences separating these three authors, the proponents of the war
between the races can be grouped into two main categories:
those, like Boulainvilliers—who in a way anticipated Joseph de
Gobineau—who postulated the permanence of the separation
between the two groups; and those, like Mably, who presupposed the fusion of the two groups. The very ambiguities in the
approach of the supporters of "fusional unity" made that approach all the more interesting. Even though they admitted the
possibility of an infiltration—a "naturalization"—of commoners of Gallo-Roman origin into the ranks of the Frankish nobility, they did not diverge from the topos of the two races.[4] The
republican position as Mably adapted it, for example, rests on a
regeneration through fusion or interbreeding, that is, on the
prior existence of two distinct races. At the heart of republican
assimilation, understood as the very constitution of a body of
citizens, lies a raciological principle centered on the mingling of
blood, though the "races" at issue in the eighteenth century had
not acquired the rigid definition that physical anthropology
later conferred on them. And, until recently, the social debate
about origins has essentially set up an opposition not so much
among aristocrats, monarchists, and republicans as between
those who believed in the original or fundamental unity of the
French people and those who assigned different origins to the
various components, regardless of whether those components
were themselves mixed.

In the first group, we may include Voltaire,[5] who harshly criticized the proponents of a Germanic origin for the nobility, and
Emmanuel-Joseph Sieyès, who recommended that the Third Estate send "all those families with the insane pretension that
they have descended from the race of conquerors back to the
forests of Franconia."[6] Nevertheless, these authors seem quite
isolated in the ocean of pluralist positions, all insisting on the
duality of the ethnic composition of the French nation.

The schema of the war between the races, adopted by the liberal historians of the Restoration and the July Monarchy, by Augustin Thierry and François Guizot in particular, found support in the new physical anthropology, which, by measuring the limbs of the human body and the volume of the brain, confirmed hypotheses regarding the origins of the different groups that supposedly compose the French population. Hence French historiography in the first half of the nineteenth century, anxious to dismiss dynastic history and to place the common people in the forefront, saw the conquered races—and therefore the Gallo-Romans—as the driving force behind the history of France. It is well known that Karl Marx's theory of class struggle was inspired by a reading of Thierry's and Guizot's works, and that, in a famous letter, Marx acknowledged the debt he owed these authors.[7] A number of Marxists have seen the race struggle as Gobineau posited it in *Essai sur l'inégalité des races humaines* (Essay on the inequality of the human races) as the monstrous avatar of a class struggle that dared not speak its name. According to them, it was, in the direct tradition of Boulainvilliers, spread by the nobles to safeguard their privileges. But we must admit, in opposition to that view of the race struggle as a deviant form of class struggle, that the war between the races is actually at the heart of the class war. That genealogy, in fact, sheds light on the fossilized notion of social class found both among Marxists such as Lenin and among established sociologists. Even the intensity of social clashes in France can be explained in part by examining them through the prism of the race struggle.

The Celtic Myth

Although the theme of the war between the races was eclipsed for a long time, a related intellectual schema took its place after the French Revolution, namely, the Celtic myth.[8] Popularized by Napoleon I, who founded the Celtic Academy in 1805, and revived by Napoleon III, that myth, designed to justify the imperial conquests, has continued since that time to develop in two different directions: the first is centered on the reunification of the different Celtic nations (Brittany, Ireland, Wales); the second makes the Gauls an entity coextensive with French national territory. It is on that last configuration that I wish to focus. Characteristically, that Gallic topos, an essential element in the definition of French identity, has been embraced virtually across the political spectrum in France. Through the figure of Vercingetorix and his exploits in Alesia and Bibracte, it inspired both Valéry Giscard d'Estaing and Jean-Marie Le Pen, both Jacques Chirac and François Mitterrand. The consensus of these major figures regarding a history of France that foregrounds the ethnic homogeneity of the nation and, as a result, establishes a radical difference between people of "French stock" and everyone else, says a great deal about the views shared by the political class as a whole, beyond the cleavage between right and left that is thought to exist within it. The permanence and predominance of the Gallic myth, beyond its folksy aspects popularized by the comic strip *Asterix*, also attest to a raciological conception of the history of France, which Le Pen articulates when he declares, for example, that the singer Patrick Bruel, alias Benguigui, is a "Gaul" or that Deputies Marcus and Dreyfus are "Romans."

When race is placed in the forefront of French national history, republican assimilation becomes a process relying on the fusion or *métissage* of the races. And, although some oppose assimilation in defense of the integrity of French identity and others favor it, both xenophobes and xenophiles agree on the existence of a French metropolitan population composed of a plurality of stocks.

The Racism of Purity, the Racism of *Métissage*

Hence the French political spectrum, rather than being sharply divided between the left and the right, can be organized along an axis with the racism of purity at one end and the racism of *métissage* at the other. At the purity end would be the National Front, a political organization contaminated by Nazi ideology and eugenics,[9] as well as part of the traditional right. At the other end is the left, and the faction of the right that can be called "republican." The racism of *métissage* or of difference thus sanctions the return in force of polygenism, that is, a plural view of human populations. That form of racism is expressed in an exemplary manner in the depiction of a multicolored France, enriched by the multiplicity of its allegiances and differences.[10] The engagement of the Senegalese infantry beside French soldiers in the trenches of Verdun, the occupation of the Ruhr by black troops after World War I, the presence of numerous West Indians, Maghrebians, and Africans on French sports teams, and even the proliferation of "multiethnic" music festivals or fashion shows illustrate the definition of a variegated France that would acknowledge itself as such, in contrast to Germany especially. That idea of a multiethnic France was the source of inspiration for the parade Jean-Paul Goude held on the Champs-Elysées on 17 July 1989 commemorating the bicentennial of the French Revolution. On that occasion, emphasis was placed on the composite nature of the French population and on something close to blood ties that unites France to its former empire. No former colonizing power has so consistently assumed responsibility for its colonial past, which allows it both to maintain its rank among nations and to assure its originality with respect to other countries. These connections, far from unilateral, are actually reciprocal, and certain countries, such as Ivory Coast and Gabon, have had as much influence on France as France has had on them.

In that sense, republicanism may entail the immoderate taste for diversity that is expressed both in the Franco-African brotherhood of "cousin" Giscard or "brother" Chirac and in the expulsion of foreigners. But the soft racism of *métissage*, as it appears, for example, on billboards advertising United Colors of Benetton, might well be a subtle way of positing irreducible differences. To postulate a palette of colors, a human variegation, is simultaneously to make assimilation or integration problematic; and, as we are now very aware, the melting pot or the republican crucible can turn out to be ineffective.

That is why, despite an outward appearance of generosity, supporters of French-style multiculturalism, by promoting "affirmative action," run the risk of creating as many difficulties as there are "target groups," which they have helped to identify and hence to produce.[11] Conversely, republican fundamentalists and relentless adversaries of the Islamic headscarf forget the constructed, historical, and shifting nature of the relation between secularism and religion and between public and private space.

In the end, the very idea of a disembodied Republic resting solely on the principle of citizenship disappears. The sense of belonging to the French nation has never been able to set aside an identification on racial—if not racist—grounds, whether in the claim to a Germanic, a Roman, or a Gallic ancestry. All the conditions for an expansion of a French-style multiculturalism seem to be converging, inasmuch as the schema of the war between the races, like the Gallic myth, clears the way for the existence of a plurality of groups. It may well be that the apex of republican secularism in the late nineteenth century only served to marginalize cultural groups by reducing the different communities to the status of private and individual religious denominations. The hardening of identities we are witnessing today, which some have called the "return of the religious," may indicate that the pendulum has now swung in the other direction. It attests, in any case, to the compatibility between the republican theory of assimilation and the existence of a plurality of groups. In this respect, G. W. F. Hegel erred in criticizing the French Revolution for its supposed desire to integrate the Jews as individuals and not as a group, since, for both the Jews and for other communities (the *Beurs*, the *harkis*, the Armenians, and so on), it was the initial identification of these minorities as ethnic groups that entitled them to be integrated into the republican body.[12]

The Human Sciences, Natural Law, and the Approach to Difference

To indicate the space where the principle of republican assimilation confronts that of difference management as it was practiced in the former French colonies and as it continues to be articulated in France, let us first evaluate how these two principles have been combined in the science claiming to study human beings in both their unity and their diversity—namely, anthropology.

Contrary to a widespread notion, anthropology is not solely the product of cultural relativism, a doctrine whose origins go back to Johann von Herder and Gottfried Leibniz, or even to Martin Luther. The tradition of *Sturm und Drang*, German nationalism, and culturalism is not the only one that can be imputed to anthropology, since that discipline is equally the heir of universalism as it was clearly expressed in the ideology of natural law, or, more generally, in the ideology of the rights of man.[1] Among the great anthropologists, these two facets appear concurrently and one can distinguish, for example, between a structuralist Claude Lévi-Strauss and a culturalist Lévi-Strauss,[2] just as one can contrast a universalistic Marshall Sahlins and a relativist Sahlins.[3]

To show how anthropology resulted from these two major currents of thought, let me first briefly indicate the genesis of natural law. Obviously, these comments in no way constitute a historical study of political thought. I simply wish to set forth a few connections between anthropology and political philosophy. I will then examine the relation between anthropology and the school of historical law.

The Genesis of Natural Law

Although specialists disagree on when the theory of natural law originated, most do agree that the seventeenth century was a critical era in the establishment of a structure essential to the functioning of our own era. To be sure, Leo Strauss believes he has found in Aristotle a doctrine positing that natural law is identical to the laws of the city; conversely, in Plato, that doctrine would be assimilated only to the absolutely just life, that is, the life of the philosopher. For the Greeks, however, not all forms of life in society occur within the city—despotism and anarchy, for example—nor do they fall within what we might call the classic conception of natural law.[4] For Strauss, it is only with Saint Thomas Aquinas that the doctrine of natural law breaks free from the hesitations found in Plato and Cicero. At that time, not only was an essential harmony between natural law and civil society posited but natural law was also endowed with immutable characteristics.[5]

By contrast, Michel Villey refuses to accept that the notion of natural law had any validity in Greco-Roman antiquity.[6] For the jurist Villey, law was certainly invented in Rome, but the form it took, namely, jurisprudence and arguments or discussions about causes, means that it cannot be assimilated to natural law. To truly be a natural law, Roman law would have had to possess a notion of the individual, which it lacked. Until the individual made its appearance, law remained confined within a holist notion of the person. For Villey, it was only with Christianity that the individual was liberated and that a sense of the liberty, equality, and fraternity of all persons emerged. Hence the modern notion of the rights of man has theological roots, even though that notion is absent from the works of Saint Thomas Aquinas. It was not until William of Ockham, Duns Scotus, and the revival of Scholasticism (Francisco de Vitoria, Hernando de Soto, Francisco Suárez, Tirso de Molina) that the first outlines of the rights of man, which would be closely associated with nominalism, were drawn.

In a recently published book, the historian of law Alain Dufour argues vigorously against that thesis of the theological origin of natural law.[7] According to Dufour, the rights of man began their rise in the seventeenth century within a totally unprecedented configuration centered on the rediscovery of Euclidean geometry, on mechanics, and, in general, on mathematics. From that perspective, Leibniz and René Descartes were the chief inspiration for the emergence of the modern idea of the rights of man, which rests on the "compositive resolution" method, that is, on an approach that first reduces reality to simple elements through analysis and then reconstructs that reality through synthesis. As a result, that method privileges deduction over induction. To adopt Leibniz's terminology in the *Monadology*,[8] it begins with the abstract universal and ends with concrete universals, thus deducing natural law through a logical operation rather than reducing it to the smallest common denominator of every legal system on the planet.

Hugo Grotius stands as the chief thinker who can be associated with the notion of modern natural law. An attorney for the Dutch East India Company, Grotius devoted his first work to the definition of seizure rights;[9] then, in a second treatise, he sought to formulate a legal doctrine of war and peace that included particular consideration of segmentary wars (*faides*).[10] Although he probably should not be seen as the forefather of modern international law,[11] Grotius, in establishing his distance from the Church and the dogma of revelation, is undoubtedly one of the authors who contributed the most to the spread of a natural law resting on "right reason" and on human "sociability."[12] Founding his approach on the physical sciences—those of Galileo—and on mathematics, he defended the idea of the secularism of natural law and even of the law's independence from the question of God's existence. Although his ideas can be linked to those of Scholasticism, his use of modern reasoning methods resolutely places him within a configuration of original thought that would accommodate all the great names of seventeenth- and eighteenth-century political philosophy.

Samuel von Pufendorf's views, like those of Grotius, developed against those propounded by theology and the dogma of revelation.[13] Pufendorf distinguished among three types of law: natural law, which is common to everyone; civil law, which is or can be different in every state; and moral theology, "so named in opposition to that part of theology in which dogmas are taught."[14] According to Pufendorf, to understand the original constitution of man, which is the foundation of natural law or of law in general, one must consider him as he is since the advent of original sin, namely, "an animal subject to a great number of wicked desires."[15] That human wickedness can be found in the "state of nature," where separate and independent families wage war on one another and live in poverty. To put an end to the "state of nature," heads of families form civil society because "if there were no justice system, they would devour one another."[16] In so doing, fathers divest themselves of their natural freedom and submit to a sovereign authority. Hence a dualist schema is established—state of nature versus civil society—that would be highly influential, in political philosophy, on John Locke and Rousseau, both of whom make reference to Pufendorf. As for Grotius, the approach that allows Pufendorf to secularize thought and to found natural law on something other than divine might depends on mathematics and, in particular, on the use Descartes made of it. That mathematical method is also at the foundation of Thomas Hobbes's political philosophy.

Hobbes assimilates man and the state to machines and grants a key place to "right reason," that is, to mathematical and deductive reason. In *Leviathan*, he contrasts two typical situations: the "state of nature" and the "Commonwealth." The "state of nature" is characterized by "a warre, as is of every man, against every man," and in that state, individuals—or families—are endowed with the right to preserve their own lives. It follows that "every man has a Right to every thing; even to one anothers body."[17] For Hobbes, the "state of nature" is partly a fiction that allows him to construct the model of the "Commonwealth" in opposition to it,[18] but he nevertheless refers several times in *Leviathan* to precise examples, such as Greece, Germania, and America.[19] In all these societies, human beings are organized into small families or seigneuries and continually wage war, an activity that, thanks to the booty it procures, promotes a system of values resting on honor. That "state of nature," moreover, continues even after commonwealths have been formed, since relations between states are still open to violence and war.[20] Even though that view of the state of nature as a state of war of "every man against every man" did not enjoy the same status as the myth of the "noble savage," it did have some effect on the development of political anthropology. Sahlins devotes a long analysis to *Leviathan* and makes the state of war "of every man against every man" the foundation for his theory of lineage as a system of predatory expansion.[21] Sahlins is one of the rare anthropologists to make explicit use of political philosophy and to trace the genealogy of anthropology—that of Marcel Mauss for example—in the works of Spinoza, Hobbes, Locke, and Rousseau.[22]

Like many political philosophers of his time, Locke also founded his approach on the "state of nature." Unlike Hobbes, however, he did not characterize it as a state of war but rather as a state of natural human sociability. True to divine and rational theology, the author of *Essay of Civil Government* hypothesized an original natural community (*communitas*) which, having fallen victim to the passions and vices of individuals, was divided into distinct societies (*civitates*) so that the prescriptions of the law of nature could be observed and peace and security could effectively reign among human beings. The concept of a "state of nature" was forged by Locke to oppose Robert Filmer's idea that patriarchy and monarchy are identical.[23] In positing that civil society is different from the state of nature, Locke also posited that monarchy obeys a different principle from that underlying the father's power over his sons. The state of nature thus has a heuristic and political function: it allows Locke to show that there are societies without a single political power or with only a temporary political power. Examples of this type of society can be found in the Old Testament and in the travel narratives of the first observers of American Indian societies. Locke quotes from a book by Father J. Acosta, a Jesuit from Peru, to support his notion of the "state of nature": "*There are great and apparent Conjectures*, says he, *that these Men*, speaking of those of Peru, *for a long time had neither Kings nor Common-wealths, but lived in Troops, as they do this day in* Florida, *the* Cheriquanas, *those of* Bresil, *and many other Nations, which have no certain Kings, but as occasion is offered in Peace or War, they choose their Captains as they please.*"[24] The existence of such societies demonstrates that one can conceive of nonabsolutist political systems where it is unnecessary to "balance" authority and where it is also possible to resist the sovereign's despotic power. Yet it is the citizen's right to resist that chiefly holds Locke's attention and, in the analysis of the conquest of England and the respective place he assigns to the Saxons and Bretons on one hand, and to the Normans on the other, we may find another figure for that right to resist. Although Locke acknowledges that governments have sometimes originated through conquest, conquest cannot be an instrument for legitimating political power. A government can exert its power effectively only by consent, and, in that configuration, the place the Saxons and Bretons occupy is the state of nature or civil society (the two terms of that opposition can easily exchange places).[25] Hence Locke invented two notions that he uses alternately to oppose absolutism and to impose the idea he is defending, that of a government resting on consent. That political formula relies both on American Indian societies and on the "natural democracy" of the Saxons. An entire school of liberal thought developed in the tradition of Locke—especially his view of the Norman conquest—and it had an influence on English and French anthropology as well (E. E. Evans-Pritchard, Meyer Fortes, Pierre Clastres).[26]

Locke, in separating patriarchal power from monarchical power and, following Grotius, Pufendorf, and Hobbes, contrasting the state of nature and the social contract, made a new field of study possible, that of kinship, and simultaneously contributed to the founding of political anthropology.[27] If, contrary to the views defended by Jean Bodin and Filmer, it is agreed that monarchy is not divine and patriarchal in its essence, then it becomes possible to distinguish between segmentary societies and state societies and to reestablish connections—as Fortes asserts—with a line of thought pursued by Aristotle in his *Politics*.[28] A discontinuity was thereby established, within which anthropological thought remains confined.

Although Rousseau's ideas on the "state of nature" are in certain respects in the direct tradition of Pufendorf, Hobbes, and Locke, they nevertheless display real differences from the notions of his predecessors. Like Locke, Rousseau maintains that the state of nature, which is a peaceful state, persists in civil society, where it governs relations between states. Similarly, he claims that conquest cannot provide legitimation for a political power and that patriarchal power differs in nature from political power.[29] But, unlike Locke, who understands the "state of nature" as an assembly of a certain number of families or "bands," Rousseau defines that state as a collection of dispersed and isolated human beings. Similarly, unlike Pufendorf and Locke, Rousseau sees primitive man as a "stupid and limited animal" who could not be governed by right reason, even though natural law is not absent from the state of nature.[30] It is from Hobbes above all that the author of *The Social Contract* takes his distance. Even though, for both Rousseau and Hobbes, the "state of nature" is governed by the law of self-preservation, that law, far from stirring human passions and wickedness, instead produces peace and compassion.[31] We know that, contrary to received wisdom, Rousseau was not the theorist of the "noble savage." Certainly, in the state of nature, man is good out of ignorance of evil, but in the "state of savagery," that of most primitive societies observable in his time, human beings are fundamentally wicked.[32] Hence the state of nature is opposed term for term to the "state of savagery," the latter constituting in some sense a degeneration of the former. The goodness of human beings in the "state of nature" is the result of uniformity, isolation, and animality—in reality, of their condition.

All these elements combined mean that, in the state of nature, human language is rudimentary; similarly, human beings have no needs, do not observe one another, and have no reason to annihilate one another since they all exist on an equal footing.[33] With technological progress, individuals organize themselves into families; their language develops; and they acquire the sense of property. The result is jealousy, passion, and the quarrels that characterize the state of savagery or "nascent society."[34] Unlike Hobbes, Rousseau therefore maintains that it is in the state of savagery, the first stage on the way to the civilized state, that "the war of every man against every man" reigns. From this perspective, conflicts among private persons are incompatible both with the state of nature and with the state of civilization; in particular, medieval duels represent a degeneration of the feudal system.[35]

For Rousseau, then, it is fitting to put an end to the instability characteristic of nascent society—an instability exacerbated by the development of private property—by establishing the civil state founded on the social contract. Through the establishment of that pact, which governs the relations between the rulers and the ruled, the "general will" will replace private interests, but without requiring that individual rights as they existed in the state of nature be abandoned.

There is no tension for Rousseau between natural right and the diversity of cultures, since the goal of the social contract is precisely to make natural law, present in the state of nature and perpetuated in a new form in nascent society, surface as well in the civil state.[36] Rousseau's view of a "state of savagery" as a state of general war and his idea of the permanence of natural law in history mean that, in more than one respect, Rousseau stands as the precursor of Mauss and Lévi-Strauss. Sahlins justifiably saw the segmentary society depicted in Mauss's *The Gift* as the equivalent of the "savage" phase in Rousseau's *Discourse on Inequality*. The establishment of the "gift," that is, of an exchange system "that extends to everything, to everyone, to all time," may be taken as equivalent to the establishment of the "social contract" governed by the "general will."[37] Schematically, this same idea can be found again in Lévi-Strauss, who, in *Tristes tropiques*, making explicit reference to Rousseau, posits "consent" and "reciprocity" as the foundation of the Nambikwara chief's power.[38] In fact, Lévi-Strauss's approach as a whole is in the direct tradition of Rousseau's political philosophy. In tracing the main lines of a program of comparative anthropology that is both structuralist and culturalist, Lévi-Strauss proposes to use the knowledge of exotic societies to define the optimal conditions for life in society. He thereby situates himself within a perspective that transcends the apparent contradictions between natural law and cultural relativism.[39]

The "Romantic Reaction" and the German School of Historical Law

What is conventionally called the "romantic reaction" did not have an exclusively German origin. Although its rise is traditionally associated with Johann von Herder, and more remotely with Gottfried Leibniz and Martin Luther, it also had representatives in England (Edmund Burke) and France (Joseph-Marie de Maistre, Louis de Bonald, Augustin Thierry). Beyond national particularities, that philosophy had a strong political coloring: it was primarily directed against the universalism of the Enlightenment, against the rights of man and the French Revolution. It found its most concrete historical manifestation in the German school of historical law.

Although Herder, in certain aspects of his works, situates himself fully within the Enlightenment current,[40] and hence within universalism, he is rightly considered one of the founders of the theory of national character (*Volksgeist*).[41] Of course, that theory was not new. Other thinkers before him, Hippocrates and Aristotle in particular, depicted the character of the different peoples of which they had knowledge and attempted to relate the characteristics of these peoples to other factors—climate, for example. The link between the theory of climate and the psychology of peoples thus became a topos of political philosophy. It is found in Montesquieu's *The Spirit of Laws*, from which Herder borrows a great deal. Herder's thought, in shifting back and forth between universalism and relativism, does not appear especially original, even though his central concept of *Volksgeist* was extraordinarily influential, not only in Germany (on Hegel) but in Europe as a whole. In *Auch eine Philosophie der Geschichte* (Another philosophy of history), Herder gave local prejudices, customs, and traditions priority over universal truths. Inspired by Leibniz, he considered different national characters to be monads that were all equally necessary and equally meritorious (*Fortgang*), and in that respect he anticipated cultural relativism. For that reason, Herder was opposed to natural law, a notion that inspired the members of the French Constituent Assembly to draw up the Declaration of the Rights of Man. He expressed his distrust of general reforms carried out in the name of reason and defended customary law against the standardization of jurisprudence. In the same spirit, his role as a pastor did not prevent him from condemning the evangelizing of primitive peoples or from praising paganism. In short, Herder was a true protoanthropologist and stands alongside Burke as one of the precursors of ethnology. As Lévi-Strauss points out, the ethnological approach "demonstrably stemmed from two harbingers. In the first place, the German historical school, from Goethe to

Fichte to Herder, gradually turned away from universalizing claims to address differences rather than resemblances, and to defend, against the philosophy of history, the rights and the virtues of the monograph. A second current originated in Anglo-Saxon empiricism as manifested in Locke and then in Burke."[42] Burke, heir to Herder and German romanticism, was especially known for his fierce opposition to the French Revolution. Against the "rights of man" demanded by reason, he set forth the rights acquired by the English over the course of their history, rights that secured them the guarantees of an already constituted "community."[43] That position made Burke a defender of rights and liberties and of the most diverse social classes and peoples (the Irish, the Hindus, the Americans); as a result, it made him a forefather of historic rights versus the aridity of the rights of man. In large measure, that protoethnological version of rights inspired the policy of army officers in India, and later, of Lord Frederick Lugard in Africa. Anxious to respect native laws, the English colonial administration drew what it needed from Burke's ideas to legitimate its practice of respecting native customs and the corollary of that practice, indirect rule.[44]

For the French, the theme of the preeminence of the rights of peoples over natural law was vigorously defended by Maistre, Bonald, and Augustin Thierry, who, in spreading the ideas of Herder and Burke, as Lévi-Strauss has noted, declared themselves proponents of a notion that granted to peoples, classes, or civil society a determining role in history.[45] Maistre, who introduced Burke's writings to France, aimed his works almost obsessively against the French Revolution and the Rights of Man. For Maistre, France's "character"—its identity—rested chiefly on three pillars: the superiority of its language, the excellence of its customs, and the legitimacy of the monarchy, which sanctioned the rights of the people.[46] Like Herder and Burke before him, the author of *Considérations sur la France*[47] maintained that there is no man in general but only Frenchmen, Italians, Russians, or Persians, whose traditions are superior to the natural law the French Revolution claimed to impose.[48] Taking the example of the Savoy, his native region, Maistre showed the aberrations resulting from the imposition of a uniform rule (the rights of man) on local customs, whose equilibrium was the result of centuries of maturation.[49]

Bonald, whom some have seen as a disciple of Maistre, was himself an ardent defender of customs and prejudices, and of the ancien régime and the place occupied within it by the Christian religion.[50] An adversary of the industrial system and nostalgic for the medieval community, he placed the family in the forefront, seeing it as the fundamental organization on which the state, religion, and the universe rest. Like Maistre, Bonald exerted a decisive influence on the rise of ethnology and sociology in France: in particular, he was the inspiration for the large-scale survey Frédéric Le Play conducted on the European family.[51]

Augustin Thierry, like the other thinkers mentioned, was an assiduous reader of Herder but also carried on the work of Boulainvilliers and comte de Montlosier, both of whom played a major role in elaborating an ethnological conception of the history of France. Known for his work on the Merovingian era[52] and on the Norman conquest of England,[53] Thierry granted priority to the history of races at the expense of individuals, and saw clashes among different ethnic groups—the Franks and the Gallo-Romans, the Normans and the Anglo-Saxons—as the key to the history of France and England. That model for reading history was applicable far beyond the borders of Europe. On one hand, it served to analyze the relation between Nilotic-Hamitic herders and Bantu peasants in East Africa;[54] on the other, Marx used it to elaborate his theory of class struggle.[55] Although Marx owed a great deal to an ethnological or romantic conception of history, he was very critical of representatives of the German school of historical law, the direct heirs of Herder's and Burke's ideas.

The German school of historical law was dominated by two major intellectual figures, Friedrich von Savigny and Jacob Grimm.[56] Savigny, a specialist in Roman law, represented a statist and authoritarian current, whereas Grimm, a Germanist, embodied a laissez-faire and communitarian perspective. In spite of their differences, Savigny and Grimm both set forth the fundamental rights of the German people against the *Aufklä-rung* and the spirit of revolutionary codification propagated by the Napoleonic conquests. At the center of their approach these two jurists and their disciples placed the notion of the people, considered a natural totality; that of customary law, conceived as the expression of the popular consciousness (*Volksgeist*); and that of organic development, viewed as the growth of natural and cultural totalities. The German school of historical law thus granted priority to the inductive or empirical method, which consists of collecting the customs of peoples and thus stands opposed to the deductive or abstract method of the proponents of modern natural law.

For Savigny, Grimm, and their emulators, there is no universal language, just as there is no law common to all peoples. In that respect, the representatives of the school of historical law truly stand as the precursors of legal pluralism, regardless of whether that doctrine was developed by jurists (Georges Gurvitch, Eugen Ehrlich), anthropologists (Max Gluckman, Leopold Pospisil), or colonial administrators (Cornelis Van Vollenhoven). That doctrine postulated that law emanates more from the national will and from civil society than from the state. Since customs are the primary source of law, it is up to jurists to compile such customs, just as literary writers and poets ought to collect the songs, proverbs, and epics of the different peoples.

Law and Anthropology

Emerging parallel to a revalorization of popular customs and traditions was the notion of an Indo-European language, and it is within this context that we need to examine the relation between law and anthropology. Nineteenth-century philologists had demonstrated that, in the final analysis, the Germanic languages were related to Greek, Latin, and even Sanskrit; Grimm maintained that there had been a very ancient form of Indo-European community, which he assimilated to the old German *mark*.[57] The *mark* was a patriarchal and democratic village where land was held and worked in common, and it represented the crucible for the political virtues of the race. That idea was transferred to England through Max Müller, a German expert in Sanskrit, who, along with English historians, hypothesized that the institution of the *mark* had been introduced to the British Isles by the Saxons.

Henry Maine, a specialist in Roman law and a disciple of Savigny, used that idea to resolve the conflict between Indian customs and British law. Working from an evolutionist perspective, he suggested that a link could be established between the laws of the different nations of the Indo-European family, a link that, in particular, connected India to Germania via Rome and England. From that point of view, British law could be seen as a developed form of Indian law and the evolution of India under the guidance of England could be compared to that of Germania under the Roman conquest.[58]

In *Ancient Law*, his first book, Maine primarily criticized the views of Hobbes, Rousseau, and Jeremy Bentham on the state of nature and individualism.[59] He expressed the idea that, unlike modern societies founded on the contract, archaic societies rested on status and patriarchy.[60] Choosing most of his examples from ancient Rome, he used the *patria potestas* as the model for patriarchy and extracted from it two forms of kinship that were to play a large role in social anthropology: cognatic kinship and agnatic kinship.[61] For Maine, Rome was the prototype of a progressive society within which it was possible to identify the different stages of legal history—legal fictions, equity, and legislation.

Parallel to his successful university career, Maine also assumed the duties of a politician and colonial administrator. In India, he was deeply involved in producing legislation and favored the freedom to enter into contracts and the expansion of individual property rights.[62] During this time, he continually established parallels between the reception of Roman law in Germany and that of English law in India.[63] When we link Maine's thought to Savigny's and to the German school of historical law, it becomes difficult to follow Fortes in situating the author of *Ancient Law* within a sociological current, which would therefore stand in contrast to a culturalist approach.[64] Of course, the distinction between societies founded on status and those resting on the contract proceeds from Locke's radical critique of Filmer's views regarding the identification of the patriarchal family with the monarchy; but Maine's fondness for collecting customs certainly stemmed from his keen interest in the German school of historical law. We must therefore turn both to natural law and to historical law in our search for the origin of "comparative jurisprudence," a discipline that, according to Fortes, is itself at the origin of kinship studies.[65]

In reality, anthropology, beyond the different origins imputed to it—natural history, the tradition of studying peoples, political philosophy, or comparative philology—has been deeply marked by the legal disciplines as a whole. Some of the founding fathers of anthropology were jurists and that orientation has been consistently maintained, particularly in Anglo-American anthropology. It was on the basis of common law that British anthropologists forged the notion of "case study" and that Gluckman and his school developed brilliant situational analyses. That legal orientation of ethnology and anthropology also influenced the discipline in France. Some academic anthropologists, Denise Paulme for example, had legal training, which led them very early on—even as their colleagues were developing indigenous cosmographies—to produce Anglo-American-style monographs.[66] Colonial administrators, who received training in which law occupied a significant place, were also led to codify "native customs" and to understand social organization in terms of rights, duties, and systems for transmitting property.[67]

It was in the area of kinship, however, that the legal disciplines had the greatest influence. Maine based his approach on the existence of a primordial patriarchy. John McLennan, also a jurist by training and influenced by Johann Bachofen's theories on mother-right, undertook a criticism of the author of *Ancient Law* by placing the emphasis on exogamy, and especially by postulating the anteriority of matriarchy. Lewis Morgan, in turn, adopted McLennan's idea and hypothesized an early "Hawaiian custom" resting on sexual promiscuity.[68] All these studies on the family, private property, and the state occupy a space marked out by jurisprudence. Hence Edward Tylor claimed that the study of questions such as exogamy did not fall within the realm of anthropology. Exogamy, he wrote, "belongs properly to that interesting, but difficult and almost unworked subject, the Comparative Jurisprudence of the lower races, and no one not versed in Civil Law could do it justice."[69]

The structural-functionalist study of kinship and marriage structures in Africa undertaken by A. R. Radcliffe-Brown and Daryll Forde are an integral part of this current.[70] In the introduction to a book intended as much for ethnologists as for "those who are responsible for formulating or carrying out policies of colonial government in the African continent," Radcliffe-Brown followed a method greatly indebted to the sciences of law but which also drew from natural history and led finally to positions not far removed from those of Lévi-Strauss in *The Elementary Structures of Kinship*. Radcliffe-Brown claimed that "an important element in the relations of kin will here be called the jural element, meaning by that relationships that can be defined in terms of rights and duties."[71] That jural orientation led Radcliffe-Brown to distinguish four types of kinship systems: systems of father-right, systems of mother-right, purely cognatic systems, and systems of dual descent. Nevertheless, though the specialist in Australian kinship systems undertook a systematic comparison of Roman law, English law, the laws of ancient Germania, and African "customs," he did not reduce kinship relations as a whole to jural relationships. Referring to Aristotle, he asserted that, in addition to justice, affection was one of the chief factors of social harmony.

That dual approach of law and sentiment is found again in one˙

of Radcliffe-Brown's best-known disciples, Meyer Fortes who, parallel to his research on the Tallensi, also engaged in a reevaluation of R. S. Rattray's works on the Ashanti.[72] Faced with the contradiction in that population between patrilineal and matrilineal principles, a contradiction Rattray understood in evolutionist terms, Fortes claims that these two principles are engaged by turns over the course of the life cycle. In the end, he distinguishes between the interests, rights, and loyalties sanctioned by law to produce good behavior and those whose strict observance rests on religion, morality, conscience, and feelings. Rights lie within the realm of corporate descent groups (matrilineages among the Ashanti, for example); affection, to use Radcliffe-Brown's term, lies rather on the side of "complementary descent."[73]

The use of the concept of "complementary descent" is an avowal of descent theory's failure to account for the functioning of segmentary societies in terms of corporate groups, that is, in legal or politico-jural terms, to use Fortes's expression. That way of understanding the group as a legal entity that can be reduced to the sum of its activities (work, ceremony, etc.) isolates these groups from one another and makes it impossible to account for their fluidity.

It is the fluidity of these groups that theorists of cognatic descent emphasize. These studies, by J. A. Barnes in particular, have sought to show that unilineal descent groups, the study of which established the success of British Africanist anthropology, cannot be found in New Guinea.[74] Functionalist anthropologists, dealing with "big men" societies, in which enterprising individuals manage to attract followers independent of lineage, have demonstrated the limit of the models created by Fortes and Evans-Pritchard but confine themselves to attributing to a particular geographical and cultural space—the societies of New Guinea—what may be imputable to gaps in the model itself. In fact, "big men" societies seem to exist in places other than New Guinea; and the Bamileke of Cameroon demonstrate that, in Africa as well, collectivities can be found whose social organization conforms poorly to the model of a segmentary society. In particular, it is possible that the commercial dynamics attributed to that population is related to the openness of the society and the capacity of its leaders to mobilize a network of dependents through personal accumulation.[75] Cognatic principles seem to be a fundamental dimension of all forms of life in society, rather than a characteristic of certain groups.

The Deductive Approach, Norm and Practice

Alliance theory, primarily associated with Lévi-Strauss, Edmund Leach, and Rodney Needham, has an advantage over descent theory in that it gives a relational identity to the group and hence does not fix it in primordialist idiosyncrasy. In making the exchange of women, goods, and services the driving force of primitive societies, alliance theorists open groups to the outside and thus grant priority to relationships over their component parts. At the same time, alliance theory undermines the foundations of inductive comparative jurisprudence and founds its approach on deduction, that is, on the regulated variation of a small number of elements, put to work, for example, in the kinship unit.[76] With the rise of structuralism, the "butterfly collection" side of anthropology disappeared in principle and a problematic broadly inspired by mathematics was set in place.[77] Nevertheless, the structuralists, though they eliminated the legalism that had permeated kinship studies, in using notions such as prescriptive marriage, preferential marriage, and jural system, apparently did not totally abandon terminology borrowed from the study of law.[78] In fact, without the assistance of statistical technologies that make it possible to keep track of marriages, technologies that were unavailable when Lévi-Strauss was composing *The Elementary Structures of Kinship*, the study of marriage would have remained at the level of norms.

The clash between norms and practices led to a response

from U.S. and British anthropologists (Scheffler, Keesing, Holy, Stuchlik), whom Michel Verdon has classified as "transaction-alists."[79] At the risk of caricature, we can characterize these authors as Benthamian anthropologists anxious to demonstrate, in any society, the law of individual profit maximization and loss minimization. The emphasis placed on the "politics of kinship" and on matrimonial strategies has represented a major advance in the study of exotic societies, even though transactionalism has in the process set aside norms and rules. Of course, social life as a whole cannot be reduced to a set of optimizable ends; and there is a margin for maneuvering and play in every system that, in particular, takes into account its transformation. If one considers every society subject to the rule of norms and does not allow a degree of freedom within every system, history becomes merely the occurrence of external events, colonial conquest among others. But it would be unfair to see the transactionalists merely as proponents of a utilitarian individuality that would subsume the plasticity of social systems. Scheffler and Keesing placed a sort of "cultural grammar" at the center of their approach, a grammar that made explicit the spectrum of identities that the social actor has the capacity to assume and select in a given situation, while recognizing that the choices are limited and not entirely arbitrary.[80]

U.S. transactionalists, returning to the idea of a code governing the behavior of social actors, deconstructed the cultural anthropology of Ruth Benedict and Margaret Mead and situated themselves within a current that could be called Saussurian and Lévi-Straussian. In so doing, they anticipated Pierre Bourdieu's criticism of Anglophone anthropologists such as J. Van Velsen, for example, who emphasized a "politics of kinship," that is, manipulation and matrimonial strategies, at the expense of social constraints and determinations.[81]

In the end, the major clash within anthropology between the proponents of norms and the supporters of practices stands as a prime example of the circle within which the discipline is enclosed. That aporia is linked, in a way that has not yet been adequately emphasized, to the place that law occupies in anthropology. In adopting a concept of norm and rule borrowed directly from positive law, anthropologists were led to argue in terms of social constraints (Durkheim), rights and duties (Radcliffe-Brown), and prescriptive models (Lévi-Strauss). That legal or legalistic inflection has spawned an opposing tendency, which insists on the vitality of practices and the margin of freedom social actors enjoy in relation to custom. The controversy between the proponents of norms and the supporters of practices thus partly intersects the debate between defenders of the notion of "agents" and supporters of the notion of "actors," or even the controversy between theorists of "order" and theorists of "change."

The "Invention of Tradition" and Its Limits

The sharp opposition between "practices" and "norms" has culminated in the idea of the creation and negotiation of tradition. Stemming from E. P. Thompson's *The Making of the English Working Class*[82] and Eric Hobsbawm and Terence Ranger's inaugural work in *The Invention of Tradition*,[83] an entire current of anthropology, based largely on the works of Jack Goody,[84] has emphasized the notion that norms, customs, and hence laws are a colonial creation. Practitioners of that current are led to see precolonial African societies as empty forms onto which the institutions of colonization would later be grafted. By means of the colonial state and its chosen instrument for intervention—writing—previously shifting practices were supposedly reified and codified, thus engendering the phenomenon of "customary law." This institution, it is claimed, was customary in name only and was in fact the result of a colonial system anxious to make customs, which would otherwise be unmanageable by a modern state, conform to the model of Roman law. We must be grateful to J. Comaroff, S. Roberts, M. Chanock, and S. F. Moore for attempting to rectify colonial ethnography and for showing that customary law is more a resource used by colonial or contemporary social actors than a fossilized institution that had perpetuated itself without variation since the precolonial period.[85] Moore, in particular, gives a precise idea of precolonial Chagga law, showing that, far from being a fixed reality, it was rather permeable to a certain number of accommodations.[86] These analyses apply to other contexts, and the data I have collected on Fulani, Bambara, and Malinké societies in southern Mali tend in the same direction.[87] Beyond that sharp opposition between the negotiable character of precolonial law and its codification in the colonial era, must we not ask the more general question of the nature of the legal? Anthropologists, both in underreaching and in overreaching, have enormous difficulties conceiving of precolonial institutions. They overreach when they conceptualize these institutions as an inverted form of modern natural law. Observing that natural law did not exist in the precolonial era, they infer that there was a legal vacuum. By turning to ancient natural law, we may be able to escape the norms/practices aporia in which anthropology—in particular the anthropology of law—has been trapped.[88]

What is to be sought in precolonial African laws may not be so much the idea of a universal custom applicable in all times, in all places, and to every person—the main characteristic of modern natural law—as a principle of order specific to a given society and aimed at assigning a place to every person within that society. Beyond the negotiable character of legal norms—a character linked to their orality—it is localism and a concern for equity that may prevail.[89] Hence the precolonial Fulani, Bambara, and Malinké societies of southern Mali seem to possess sets of decentralized norms, but the variations in "custom" do not irremediably subject individuals to mere arbitrariness. Similarly, hierarchy—that is, the concern to take human differences in aptitude, means, and condition into account—does not seem to have prevented an egalitarian principle from being expressed. The new Anglophone anthropology of law, in emphasizing the negotiation of legal norms and, consequently, the invention of customary law in the modern era, has privileged practices over rules. But we ought not to conclude that, because a society does not possess writing—or because writing occupies only a marginal place in it—there is no principle of order. The criteria of good and evil, true and false, just and unjust, and the principles of social organization and the hierarchization of social status attest to the fact that illiteracy is not synonymous with anarchy and that, in the absence of a formal legal system, a set of norms exists in the societies studied by ethnologists.

In addition, in order for imported written laws to penetrate these societies, there must be an underlying structure, a normative infrastructure on which a legal code can be grafted. Without falling into legalism and thus seeing any custom whatsoever as a protolaw, we need to recognize the universality of norms and rules, a universality that indigenous theories take into account. Nevertheless, beyond the recognition of that universal principle, it is difficult to deduce the characteristics of different societies, which remain confined within their splendid isolation; in this respect, deductive natural law is not of much help. Comparative jurisprudence, with its parade of "customaries," also does not appear very useful, since it serves to transform the normative into the legal. Only an inventory of concepts seems capable of providing the tool able to delimit spaces within which the variation of one or several themes can be analyzed.

Anthropology often overreaches, but it may also underreach, by ignoring such precolonial forms of written law as Muslim law. These types of law may not be strictly identical to our written laws, and the "justice of the qadi" may be somewhat different from that administered by our judges, but that is no justification for anthropologists to have ignored them or for the colonial administration to have disregarded them, especially when the societies being studied or administered were reputed to be pagan.[90]

The question of comparing kinship and alliance systems within a given cultural zone—in this case, the Fulani, Bambara,

Malinké, Senufo, and Minyanka zone in southern Mali and in the northern part of Ivory Coast—thus takes on the appearance of a metaphysical discussion if the presence of a major element, the influence of Muslim law, is not taken into account. For example, if one opposes Senufo matrilinearity to Bambara patrilinearity or Minyanka direct exchange to Malinké generalized exchange, one judges these societies in essentialist terms and fails to see them as systems of transformation. To differentiate these societies on the basis of mother-right versus father-right, or sister exchange versus dowry exchange, that is, to reintroduce Maine's and Radcliffe-Brown's old jural problematic, is to avoid taking into account the existence of a cultural continuum within which Islam serves a function.[91]

From direct exchange to marriage with dowry to Arab marriage, it is the adoption of Islam, not an unchanging membership in a given society, that has brought about the shift from one matrimonial system to another.[92] The spectrum of kinship and marriage systems in that region must be understood as a function of a gradual growth in the practice of Islam, and not in terms of rigid typologies. It is by playing on a shared but already diversified foundation of customs, practices, and norms that Muslim law brought about a demarcation between related social systems, a demarcation that colonial codification subsequently reinforced. Only by disregarding the influence of Islam were colonial administrators and ethnologists able to divide these systems into a series of discontinuous entities.

Anthropologists, in moving beyond natural law on one hand and comparative jurisprudence on the other, will be able to identify a world view within exotic societies, a set of concepts and norms that give these societies the means for their reproduction.

Whether or not these means are associated with a written culture, there is something normative, if not legalistic, in any human society, and it is difficult to imagine a collectivity that would not be governed by any ordering principle. The error of the proponents of natural law has been to analyze the concepts and norms of exotic societies only in rational and individualistic terms. Symmetrically, the proponents of comparative jurisprudence have delighted in coming up with a global list of rules, leaving aside local variations in norms among contiguous societies and ignoring written precolonial laws.

It is, therefore, by adopting a middle position between universalism and culturalism—that is, by broadening the horizon of local societies and by practicing a moderate comparativism—that anthropology will be able to escape the sharp opposition between norms and practices, order and change, actors and agents.

The definition of the anthropological space—especially the French anthropological space—within which the proponents of culturalism and those of relativism face off, makes it possible to establish the foundations for an analysis of the relation between the application of natural law and the management of difference during the various French colonial enterprises. It was in the colonies, in fact, that the dominance of these two theories took root, affecting not only the social sciences in France but also the very existence of the different communities making up French national territory.

The Origins of French Multiculturalism: The Egyptian Expedition

An effort was made to organize a government of the natives by the natives.

> —Louis Reybaud, *Histoire scientifique et militaire de l'expédition française en Egypte*

The Egyptian expedition, the first colonial enterprise subsequent to the Enlightenment and the French Revolution, was a true laboratory for French expansionism in the nineteenth century. It was exemplary in that it rested on three contradictory but closely interrelated theories: the theory of regeneration, the theory of natural law, and the theory of racial and linguistic classification. These theories can be observed at work throughout the period of French colonization.[1]

Through the Egyptian expedition, a project of "rational" colonization took shape that was aimed at developing the conquered societies by using the combined insights of relativism and universalism. Hence there was an effort both to individualize the different peoples and to conceptualize cultural difference in terms of developmental delay. The heuristic aspect of that expedition is clear to anthropologists, who reflect on the archaeology of their discipline and strive to link that discipline to development efforts. For Africanists, the Egyptian expedition also has a demonstrative value, in that it constituted the foundation on which French domination was built in sub-Saharan Africa. After all, did not Bonaparte see the takeover of Egypt as the key to French penetration into black Africa?[2]

Regeneration

As Mona Ozouf has shown in *L'homme régénéré*,[3] the entire eighteenth century was permeated with the idea of a "second birth," an idea embodied in a series of figures such as the wild man of the woods, the marooned man of the Canary Islands, and the blind man who recovers his sight. The Enlightenment thus intended to create a new people or, more exactly, a "brand-new people." It was believed that this brand-new people had been found in what in France were considered at the time to be "lost lands"—the islands, moors, and deserts—but also in regions with enigmatic languages—the Basque region, for example— places without priests, administrators, or laws, without locks and keys, where there were neither masters nor slaves. It was also believed that this new people could be identified in the populations of which the ancients had spoken, such as the Lacedaemonians, the Cretans, or the Greeks.

Ideal characteristics were attributed to these new tribes: they were small and scattered. Their members constantly interacted with one another; they maintained a sort of moral sociability and had no needs. The revolutionaries believed that it was by becoming like these brand-new ancient peoples that they had some chance of recovering the humanity within themselves.

These ideas took on a particular coloring with Abbé Grégoire, author of a book significantly titled *Essai sur la régénération physique, morale et politique des juifs* (Essay on the physical, moral, and political regeneration of the Jews).[4] Abbé Grégoire militated strongly for the emancipation of the Jews in France, the blacks in Africa, and the slaves in the West Indies. He intended to have the Jews enter civil society by allowing them access to all trades, by favoring mixed marriages, and by obliging them to abandon those customs that were in contradiction with the laws of the nation. Hence, "castes" and "ethnicities," which threatened the homogeneity of French society, would disappear. Similarly, he intended to put an end to the tyranny oppressing the Africans and West Indians by spreading the enlightenment of reason and Christianity among them, by favoring mixed unions, and by ensuring the development of their economies.[5]

From that perspective, it was fitting, more broadly, to foster the improvement of the common people or Third Estate. In the tradition of ancien régime historiography, the common people were seen as descendants of the conquered race—the Gallo-Romans—and the nobility were considered the heirs of the Franks, conquerors from Germania. The fusion of these two races in the French melting pot was supposed to assure republican assimilation. The regeneration of the common people thus depended on their emancipation, that is, on their disappearance as a race and their fusion with the republican political body through the elimination of despotism.

These ideas did not apply solely to the history of France: Constantin Chasseboeuf, comte de Volney, for example, Grégoire's friend and one of the chief inspirations for Bonaparte and members of the Egyptian expedition, also transferred them to the history of the East.[6] For Volney, the idea of regeneration needed to take root in the East because despotism, fanaticism, and the ignorance of natural law reigned in that part of the world. For him, the general degradation of the human race in those parts was not due, as it was for Montesquieu, to the pernicious climate, supposedly a powerful and immutable factor, but to Eastern despotism, which left the common people to stagnate and made that region a backward zone in comparison to Europe.[7] When the people had been liberated from despotism, the East's political backwardness in relation to the West would be overcome. The theory of race, transformed into a theory of class, thus made it possible to solve the problem of archaic ways. According to Volney, the East's cultural backwardness was of a political nature; it was not racial or ethnic. There was no cultural specificity or relativism in his philosophy, only a sociological relativism: hence the need for outside intervention, which would liberate the peoples of the East from despotism.

Volney's republican imperialism was based both on the spread of natural law and on the theory of invasions and races.[8] That is why, though an ardent defender of natural law and of human identity across time and space, he also favored the creation of museums of ethnography and was respectful of the specificity of each culture.[9] Natural law, far from standing in opposition to race theory, thus appeared as its corollary, since that principle, which lay within the people and was stifled by despotism, had to be revived.

Bonaparte, who met Volney before leaving for Egypt, was greatly inspired by him to undertake the expedition that led him to the banks of the Nile. Volney's *Voyage en Egypte et en Syrie* (Journey to Egypt and Syria) was the French expedition's guide; and, on his return to Cairo, Bonaparte went to congratulate Volney for his perspicacity and his knowledge of the East. Hence, far from blindly applying natural law, Bonaparte and his army, in formulating their plan for the conquest and administration of Egypt, depended on the knowledge accumulated by Volney during his travels to the East.

Philhellenism—that is, the doctrine that legitimated the Europeans' support of the Christian Greeks against their Muslim Turk oppressors—was also one of the major intellectual sources of the Egyptian expedition.[10] Corresponding to the opposition between the Greeks and the Turks established by that doctrine was the cleavage between the ruled Arabs and the ruling Ottomans. In the minds of the members of the Egyptian expedition, Arab history had known a time of splendor during the early centuries of Islam, before sinking into continuous decline as a result of the combined inadequacies of military despotism and religious despotism, both of which were characteristic of Turk-

ish domination. During their age of splendor, the Arabs had perfected the Greeks' science and had transmitted it to the West.
The Western rationalism that the French expeditionary corps
delivered to the East was a return of science to its native country.[11]

In the direct tradition of philhellenism, the French portrayed
the conquest of Egypt as a liberation of the peoples of the East
from their local despots, the Mamluks, and more generally,
when all hope of reaching terms with the Porte had vanished,
from Ottoman domination.[12] The future of Egypt and of the
Eastern world could lie only in the nation-state and in the recovery of the pharaonic ideal. The process of civilization was to
come about through regeneration. After Bonaparte became emperor, he continued to use the term "civilization" to justify his
Mediterranean policy of regeneration in Italy and Spain.

In Egypt, the French conquerors set up an opposition between
the Bedouin Arabs, the victims of despoliation, and their Mamluk and Ottoman oppressors. From that perspective, regeneration and national recovery depended on the eradication of the
local despotic structure, represented by these two categories of
leaders. That policy of dividing Egyptian society into two antag-
onistic groups did not have the anticipated effect and the invasion of the French army led rather to the unification of Egyptians
as a whole against the invader. The enterprise of "deculturaliz-
ing" Egyptian society was thus a failure and that society re-
sponded to the invaders by sending back a unitary image of itself.
That image may lie at the origin of the accusation of "textual-
ization" that some people have leveled at Orientalism.[13]

Natural Law

The idea of a deductive natural law, valid for everyone in
every time and place, gradually emerged in Western thought and
lay at the root of the American and French Revolutions. Although it is possible to debate the origin of the 1789 Declaration

of the Rights of Man and of the Citizen (Locke or Rousseau?),[14] that natural law clearly inspired the first colonial expedition conducted in the name of the Enlightenment.[15] How could natural law have justified an enterprise of conquest? As F. Gauthier has shown, it was the slow degradation of the principles of natural law over the course of the revolution that accounts for that phenomenon.[16]

In fact, although both Declarations of the Rights of Man and of the Citizen (1789 and 1793) were founded on natural law, the Constitution of 1791 represented a first attack on that principle, an attack that intensified with the Constitution of 1795. The latter constitution, which no longer referred to a law common to all men, set forth the rights and duties of man in society.

The clash between the proponents of natural law and the supporters of a notion granting complete self-determination to only a fraction of humanity, turned essentially on slavery and the relations—egalitarian or nonegalitarian—that ought to exist between peoples. Although the Constitution of 1793 abolished slavery and the Constitution of year III upheld that abolition, a distinction was now established between physical freedom and political independence. That distinction made it possible to legitimate the colonial conquests and opened the way for what would be a very influential theme, namely, assimilation.[17] In the debates on slavery that took place at the Constituent Assembly between May and September 1791, Jean-Siffrein Maury distinguished three categories within colonial society: the white settlers, the "countless tribe" of black laborers constituting the foreigners, and, between them, the métis and the emancipated slaves, who formed an intermediate group destined to be "assimilated" after a long probation period. The Egyptian expedition can be situated within that context of a progressive limitation of natural law, which culminated in 1802 with Bonaparte's reinstitution of slavery.

Volney shared that hesitation between a humanist and universalist conception of natural law and a more restrictive notion of the rights of man. In his desire to see natural law applied to humanity as a whole, and in particular to the peoples of the East, he saw European intervention as the only solution.[18] For Volney, the promotion of natural law, or more exactly, of natural laws, was intimately connected to that of "regeneration." In order for Eastern societies, particularly Egypt, to recover their bygone splendor, it was necessary to extend to that region of the world a principle that had its birth in the West but which ought to be universally applied, since the Enlightenment postulated the identity of all men across time and space. Natural laws, as Volney understood them, were modeled on physical laws.[19] They thus took on a scientific character but were also primordial and consistent with human nature; hence, if they were applied, the conformity of all social contracts—or "conventions"—and the prosperity of humanity could be guaranteed.[20] With that approach, Volney situated himself in the tradition of eighteenth-century political philosophy and of Rousseau's ideas in particular, even though he was a declared adversary of the author of the *Social Contract*, and especially of the Edenic vision of primitive man that he thought he detected in Rousseau.[21]

It was in the prophecies contained in his book *Ruines* that Volney's notions relating to natural law were best expressed, notions that were to spread throughout the world.

> O kings and priests, you can suspend for a time the formal publication of the laws of nature, but it is not in your power to destroy or overturn them. . . . Seek out the laws to lead us that nature has placed within you, and build the authentic and immutable code from them; but may they no longer be for a single nation, for a single family; may they be for all without exception! Be the lawmaker of the entire human race, as you will be the interpreter of that same nature; show us the line that separates the world of chimera from the world of realities, and teach us, after so many religions and errors, the religion of evidence and truth![22]

That philosophy of natural laws was not only an abstract principle; it also had an application in the economic realm, where it served to legitimate the right to property.[23] These principles would be adopted as such by Bonaparte, who was a fervent admirer of Volney, and they made it possible to introduce deep reforms in Egyptian land tenure.

Raciological and Linguistic Classifications

The raciology associated with linguistics was in some sense the crowning achievement of the scientific edifice built up around the Egyptian expedition. Here again, Volney influenced every view expressed regarding the settlement of the banks of the Nile. Volney's depiction of the population in *Voyage en Egypte et en Syrie* was a direct extension of the theory of the two races, a theory that continued to provide the paradigm used to analyze the history of France. Influenced by Boulainvilliers and Mably, Volney set up a general opposition between the conquerors and the conquered. He also wondered how much *métissage* had occurred between these strata of the population and, correlatively, whether it was possible to observe races and languages that had not been altered by such mingling. For him, that question was strategic because it determined the country's political regime and made it possible to reconstitute its history.[24] On the basis of that general interpretive framework, he analyzed the different strata of Egyptian society and took an inventory of the ethnic groups composing it. For the author of *Ruines*, social and racial classification went hand in hand; in that respect, he was Montesquieu's successor and Thierry's precursor. Volney distinguished four races within the Egyptian population: the Arabs, the Copts, the Turks, and the Mamluks. For him, however, the initial opposition lay between the Arabs and the Copts, since the Turks and Mamluks represented much more recent population strata. Unlike Georges Buffon, who classified the population of North Africa and Egypt within the white race, Volney made the Copts part of the black race.[25]

He saw the Copts as descendants of a stratum of early occupiers, who had been subjugated by the Arab conquerors. Endowed with particular racial characteristics, the Copts also

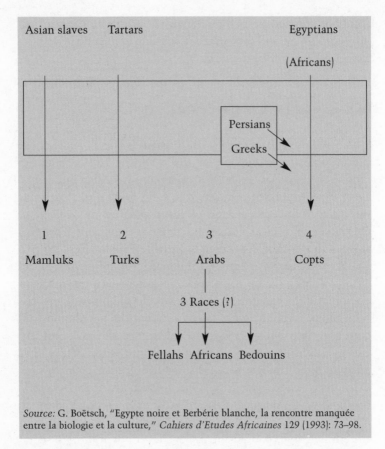

Source: G. Boëtsch, "Egypte noire et Berbérie blanche, la rencontre manquée entre la biologie et la culture," *Cahiers d'Etudes Africaines* 129 (1993): 73–98.

Figure 1. Ethnogeny of the Four Races of Egypt according to Volney

possessed a language of their own. That language, related to ancient Greek and Egyptian, displayed striking resemblances to the languages of other peoples in the region: in particular, the Arabs, the Ethiopians, the Syrians, and the inhabitants of the banks of the Euphrates.[26] After their idiom was supplanted by Arabic, the Copts preserved only their religion, and placed themselves in the service of the Ottomans and Mamluks.[27]

Volney did not originate the thesis that attributed a black origin to Egyptian civilization: he merely adopted for his own purposes the point of view of Herodotus and of Diodorus Siculus, who had already pointed out that Egypt was settled by blacks. But Volney added an eighteenth-century—that is, a scientific—touch to a very ancient view, and it is for that reason that his views have been well received by Afrocentrist ideologues such as Cheikh Anta Diop or M. Bernal, who vigorously defend the theory of the black African origin of Egyptian civilization.[28]

It was also Volney's racial classification and the idea that the Copts were the "former indigenous people" of Egypt that led Bonaparte to form a Coptic legion under the command of General Jacob.[29] In addition, Napoleon's preferred policy of divide and conquer led the emperor to rely on other ethnic minorities, especially Jews and other Christians.

The general intellectual configuration governing the Egyptian adventure thus made it possible to reconcile two a priori irreconcilable principles: natural law and raciology. In introducing a scission within the conquered populations, in breaking them down to their different components, it was possible to foster a resurgence of natural law, buried within the healthy elements, that is, the common people. Once the intellectual obstacles to establishing that policy had been removed, the policy could be applied, though only at a high cost.

The Conquest and Administration of Egypt

The conquest of Egypt by Bonaparte's troops occurred within the context of a slow decline of Ottoman power that had begun in the seventeenth century, a decline concretely marked by the drop in the tribute sent to Constantinople and, correlatively, by the rise in power of the Mamluks, slave warriors of Georgian or Circassian origin.[30]

In Egypt before the conquest, social competition centered primarily on buying up urban and rural tax farms (*iltizam*), which harmed taxpayers and the Ottoman treasury alike. Rivalries internal to the ruling stratum were stirred up by Constantinople, which was attempting to maintain its control over the banks of the Nile. The regime in power was divided into camps or parties, each attracting Mamluk beys, militias, urban supporters, and Bedouin confederations. The Mamluks monopolized all official positions, both in the administration and in the militias, and their omnipresence in the state apparatus was expressed in a growing exploitation of urban artisans and merchants.

In rural areas, the tax farm system prevailed. In exchange for an advance on the tax (*miri*) owed the state, the tax farmer (*multazim*) received usufruct of a portion of the public lands. The rural tax farms were the source of the Mamluks' power: the Mamluks controlled nearly two-thirds of them.

Since the *multazim* generally lived in town, the lands were managed by the most important peasant in the village community, the *shaykh al-balad*, or village chief, who, by distributing and collecting taxes, was in charge of the entire system of exploitation of village land. The state, which had no direct contact with the peasant world, was represented in the rural areas by the *shaykh al-balad*, but the *multazim* shielded the *shaykh al-balad* from the rest of the administrative system, an arrangement that increased the tax burden on the peasants. In addition, levies were imposed by the Bedouins in the area, who ravaged Upper Egypt and the edges of the Nile delta.

By the late eighteenth century, the rural areas were experiencing constant political instability: the peasants were victims of the devastation perpetrated by the Mamluk factions and by the Bedouins. An alliance between the ulema (notables) and the common people was formed to respond to that oppression; it opposed the Mamluks and was encouraged by the Ottoman powers. Bonaparte and his army, by playing on the rivalry between the common people, the ulema, and the Ottoman on one hand and the Mamluks and Bedouins on the other, attempted to establish their power base in Egypt.

In the days preceding the landing in Alexandria, Bonaparte, with the cooperation of Venture de Paradis, an Orientalist dragoman, drafted a proclamation to the Egyptian people in which he attempted to present himself as someone who had come to end the iniquities committed by the Mamluks and to restore the legitimate Muslim authority.

> In the name of God the benefactor, the merciful, there is no god but God; there are no sons or partners sharing his dominion. On behalf of the French Republic founded on liberty and equality, General Bonaparte, head of the French army, informs the people of Egypt that for too long the beys that govern Egypt have insulted the French nation and snubbed its merchants: the time for their punishment has come. For too long, that pack of slaves purchased in the Caucasus and Georgia have tyrannized the greater part of the world; but God, the Lord of worlds, the omnipotent, has commanded that their empire shall end.
>
> Egyptians, you will be told that I have come to destroy your religion: do not believe it! Reply that I have come to restore your rights against the usurpers, that I have more respect for the Mamluks, for God and his prophet, Muhammad, and for the glorious Koran. Tell them that all men are equal before God and differ only in wisdom, talent, and virtue. But what wisdom, what talent, what virtue distinguish the Mamluks that they should hold exclusively everything that makes life sweet and dear? . . . God is just and merciful toward the people; and with the aid of the Almighty, beginning today, no Egyptian will be prevented from having access to high office: let the wisest, the best-educated, and the most virtuous govern, and the people will be happy.
>
> There were once great cities, great canals, great commerce among you: what destroyed everything, if not the avarice, the injustice, and the tyranny of the Mamluks? Qadis, sheikhs, shorbagi, tell the people that we are true Muslims. . . . Conversely, have not the Mamluks always revolted against the authority of the Great Lord, whom they still do not recognize? . . . Thrice blessed will be they who are with us! . . . But woe, woe to those who arm themselves in support of the Mamluks and fight against us! . . .
>
> Article 1: All villages located within a radius of three

leagues from the places the army will pass through will send a delegation to the general commanding the troops, to alert them that they swear their allegiance, and that they have hoisted the army's white flag (white, blue, red).

Article 2: All villages that take up arms against the army will be burned.

Article 3: All villages that submit to the army will place, alongside the flag of the great sultan our friend, that of the army.

Article 4: The sheikh will have the goods, houses, and property belonging to the Mamluks placed under lock and key and will take care that nothing is misappropriated.

Article 5: The sheikhs, the qadis, and the imams will continue in the duties of their offices: every resident will stay home and prayers will continue as usual. Everyone will thank God for the destruction of the Mamluks and will shout: Glory to the Sultan, glory to the French army, his friend! Woe to the Mamluks and blessed be the people of Egypt.[31]

Four main themes can be drawn from this proclamation: the restoration of the legitimate Ottoman authority and the correlative destruction of the despotism of the Mamluks—"that pack of slaves purchased in the Caucasus and Georgia," who limited freedoms and brought about the ruin of the country; the French people's allegiance to Islam based on the call for a struggle against the enemies of Islam (the Catholic Church); the regeneration of the "Egyptian people," that is, the advancement of individuals solely as a function of their merits; and finally, the establishment of a Muslim policy, which is simultaneously a policy of notables.

Whereas the first two points seem to be circumstantial arguments, the last two stem from the principles that guided the French expedition's actions throughout its time in Egypt. But is it not contradictory simultaneously to call for regeneration—an idea based on natural law and rationalization—and to set in place a policy based on Islam and notables? Is there not a clash between introducing a great program of civilization and reform and the daily constraints involved in administering an unfamiliar country stubbornly resistant to foreign occupation?

Two major tendencies seemed to take shape in the oversight set up in Egypt by the French between 1798 and 1801: rational administration and cultural administration.

Rational Administration

For the anniversary celebration of 13 Vendémiaire (4 October 1798), Bonaparte gave the following speech: "We offer the world the first example of a *conquering lawmaker* [my emphasis]. Until now, conquerors have always adopted the laws of the conquered. Let us secure the victory of reason over them, a victory more difficult than that of arms, and let us show ourselves as superior to other nations as Bonaparte is superior to Genghis Khan."[32]

These few sentences express the radical originality of the Egyptian expedition when compared to previous colonial conquests. Bonaparte and his army clearly proclaimed the need to establish a rational body of laws that would leave only limited room for local customs. It is not difficult to find, among the reforms undertaken by the French conquerors, a whole series of measures inspired by reason and natural law. That desire to rationalize Egyptian society applied not only to the realm of law and administration; it also affected other sectors such as health, women's condition, and economic development, for example.[33]

It was the principle of regeneration that guided the French in their effort to modify Egypt's social fabric, and the application of that principle presupposed eliminating the despotism embodied by the Mamluks or, more generally, by the leisure classes. As 'Abd Allāh Menou, the last commander in chief of the French expeditionary corps, declared, that meant "elevating the hard-working class of fellahs [peasants]," thus assuring economic development by limiting "the influence of powerful people . . . who . . . have constantly crushed the common people, who bear almost the entire burden of taxation."[34]

The aim of that precursor to the "direct contact" policy was to link the French to the Egyptian masses and, in the end, to assure the fusion of the two peoples within a new society.[35] That policy was applied to two main areas: the tax system and the judicial system.

The Tax System

In the declaration he made upon landing in Alexandria, Bonaparte granted a significant place to a policy centered on the use of Islam and the use of notables, that is, to a mode of cultural or indirect administration inspired by Orientalists such as Volney and Venture de Paradis. That was the context for the creation of the divan (council) of Cairo and the provincial divans. At the same time, however, recourse to the ulema and the local sheikhs was constantly limited by measures restricting or totally abolishing their power, for example, during the period following the Cairo revolt, when a true regime of rational or direct administration was adopted. As Reybaud remarks: "The essential thing was thus to give it [the divan] leadership from afar, to use Egyptian names to govern in the French manner."[36]

In fact, the heads of the French expeditionary corps persistently tried to accustom notables to the ideas of assembly and government prevailing in France.[37] Hence they decided that the sheikhs of the divan would draw salaries whereas, under the Ottomans, they were remunerated by tax revenues. Similarly, they required that members of the divan provide advances on revenue from the largest farms (*iltizam*). In general, the organization of the Egyptian tax system, which relied on tax farmers (*multazim*), was also constantly being reformed. Under Menou, these reforms culminated in the complete disappearance of the *multazim*. In fact, the tax levies carried out by the *multazim*— usually Mamluks—were considered iniquitous by the French, who saw them as among the sources of Oriental despotism.

In place of that archaic institution they attempted, first, to set in place a system with a staff composed half of Frenchmen and half of Copts. The latter were judged indispensable because of their knowledge of the country. Later, a European-style tax system was created, which relied on a property records office, a cadastre, a tax on real property, a direct tax, and new customs duties. In the spirit of that reform, taxation was modernized through the establishment of new levies and the individualization of those already in existence. Hence the French believed that the *beit el-mal* represented an arbitrary inheritance tax and decided to replace it with an individual tax respecting everyone's rights and duties.

In the rural areas, reform consisted essentially of eliminating the *multazim* and making the *shaykh al-balad* and members of the provincial divan the collectors of funds. That measure gradually transformed the *shaykh al-balad* into civil servants and made the state the authorized representative of the upper stratum of rural society, at the expense of the Mamluks. Similarly, thanks to the oversight the French exercised in the rural areas, the Bedouin levy disappeared, putting an end to one of the numerous exactions of which the peasants had been victims.

All these measures were dictated by the concern to eliminate the burdens on the exploited peasant class and by the desire to establish the right to individual property. By setting in place the principles of natural law and the regeneration of the people, the French intended to reconcile economic equity with development. These principles were also at work in the area of the justice system.

The Judicial System

Believing that the Muslim justice system was governed by custom and that the qadis (Muslim judges) were all-powerful and corrupt, the French intended to eradicate "barbarian" or "despotic" practices and to establish true law.[38] In that respect, the attitude of members of the expeditionary corps toward Muslim jurisprudence and, in particular, toward the custom known as "blood price" (*diyya*) was exemplary. They were stunned to discover that murders resulting from quarrels between families did not end with the condemnation and execution of the murderer, as was done in France, but rather with the payment of a sum of money to the victim's family. They first proposed to abolish that "barbarous" practice. Subsequently, under Menou, the custom was replaced by a French-style penal procedure. On the whole, the Egyptian justice system evolved toward more active involvement by the conquerors.[39]

The commerce tribunal, for example, assumed jurisdiction over matters of personal status, one of the most fundamental areas of Islamic law. Similarly, the judicial commission designed to judge crimes compromising public safety included members who were French officers, and death sentences could be pronounced only with the approval of the general in chief. Finally, under Menou, the duties of the divan were reduced to those of a simple appeal tribunal for the indigenous people.

The French attributed barbarous customs such as "blood price" to the despotism, fanaticism, and ignorance supposedly characteristic of Muslim jurisprudence and not to the relativism of values. The establishment of a justice system based on natural law, and hence on equality before the law, was to allow them to eliminate practices of another era and to abolish the abuses of the Ottoman justice system. The famous chronicler Abd al-Rahman al-Jabarti, though he admired the conquerors' justice system, had few illusions about the meaning of French intervention.[40] He was not unaware that Bonaparte's officers reserved for themselves control of important affairs and delegated their power to the divan only for minor matters.

The denigration of custom and its use only for petty purposes were merely two aspects of the same phenomenon, and it was within that perspective that the field of cultural administration was defined in Egypt.

Cultural Administration

In 1788 Volney had warned Bonaparte that, to "establish oneself in Egypt, one would have to prosecute three wars: the first against England, the second against the Porte, and the third, the most difficult of all, against the Muslims, who constitute the population of that country. That war will produce so many losses that it must perhaps be considered an insurmountable obstacle."[41] As soon as Bonaparte arrived in Cairo, he took Volney's advice and, with the help of Venture de Paradis, set in place an Islamic policy relying on the use of notables.[42] At the same time, he strove to promote the Jewish, Greek, and Coptic minority communities. It was on these two pillars that the indirect or cultural systems of taxation and justice established by the French expeditionary corps rested.

The Tax System

Even though the French were eager to reform—in time—the Egyptian tax system as a whole and to found it on the principle of natural law, they rapidly became aware that it was impossible to completely overhaul the Mamluk or Ottoman system. That system was extremely complex; in fact, the French called it "feudal."[43]

Within that system, the peasant farmed for his own gain in exchange for a fixed fee that he paid the owner in cash or in kind. That fee was subdivided into three major categories: the *miri*, the property tax owed to the lord of the manor or to the state; the *fayz*, which was set aside for the owner; and the *barrany* or *mudaf*, a supplementary tax to pay for any extraordinary expenses.[44]

Given the intricacies of the Mamluk tax system, the French were obliged to enlist the services of Coptic auxiliaries, the only ones capable of collecting the taxes. Under Bonaparte, then, Coptic intendants were first charged, under the supervision of French agents, with advancing the totality of the taxes owed to occupation authorities, and were then responsible for recovering it subsequently from the peasants. But the effect of that policy of farming out taxes, which was also a policy for promoting minorities, sowed discontent among the Egyptian population. Later, after Bonaparte's departure, Jean-Baptiste Kléber therefore attempted to restrict the role of the Copts. The general in chief combined all taxes into one but nevertheless continued to make the Copts responsible for recovering it, in exchange for an 8-percent cut. Even under Menou, the French, though they wanted to put an end to the despotic character of the Egyptian tax system, never succeeded in doing without the Copts completely or in establishing a tax system based on natural law.[45]

The Judicial System

In the area of justice, Bonaparte's policy of indirect administration essentially consisted of creating the divan of Cairo and the divans of the provinces, authorities charged with creating a buffer between the "natives" and the French expeditionary corps.

The divan of Cairo was composed of sixty members, including fourteen permanent ones. The permanent members were recruited among the sheikhs and merchants, to the exclusion of the Mamluks.[46] The *dhimmi,* that is, Coptic and Syrian Christians, were also represented, as were the Europeans (the English, Swedes, and French). The presence of French representatives such as Gaspard Monge and Claude-Louis Berthollet, who were backed by Venture de Paradis and the other dragomans, made possible the oversight of that indigenous authority.

In the provinces, the divans were composed of ulema, who replaced the Ottomans in that function, and by merchants and *shaykh al-balad.* In addition, this council was assigned a police force, which was recruited from the janissary corps. The members of these provincial divans, which were placed under close French supervision, sent a deputation to the divan of Cairo composed of three men of law, three merchants, three fellahs, and a number of *shaykh al-balad* and Arab chiefs.

The role the French assigned to the provincial divans was also primarily to oversee tax collection and the administration of justice. Under the French occupation, the Egyptians were governed by Islamic tribunals and remained subject to the application of the Shari'a (Koranic law). The divan of Cairo, like the provincial divans, thus administered justice in accordance with a three-tiered procedure, which al-Jabarti has described.[47] Plaintiffs who came before these tribunals presented their cases, which the interpreter then translated into French. If the case fell within the jurisdiction of the Shari'a, the qadi settled the matter based on the opinion of the ulema; if necessary, a request was made to the great qadi of the tribunal for authentic written proof, so that the record could be set straight. If the complaint did not fall within Koranic law—in the case of farm rents, for example—the matter was transferred to the French. In that way, the French increased the power of Islamic tribunals since, before their takeover of the country, death sentences were reserved for the Mamluks' direct justice and were not decided by the qadis. Conversely, the autonomy granted to the Egyptian legal authorities rapidly reached its limits, since in cases of an offense compromising public safety, or when the commander of the province decided to refer the matter to a French tribunal, a legal commission made up of French officers was formed. In addition, death sentences could be carried out only with the approval of the general in chief.

The French thus delegated their power to the Egyptians for minor matters because they were not numerous enough to control the country as a whole, as attested in the appointment of Mourad Bey to the emirate of Upper Egypt.[48] Whenever serious matters were at stake or their safety was threatened—after the revolt of Cairo, for example—they took things into their own hands and shifted to a system of direct administration.

In the following passage, Reybaud describes the ambiguous nature of the powers of the divan of Cairo:

In all matters of detail regarding the policing of Cairo, Mohammadan ritual, the mores and customs of the country, and the basis of taxes, Poussielgue and Dugua [the French representatives] required the divan's mediated or unmediated intervention. The Muslim assembly, implicated thereby in everything that was done, offered the support afforded by its popularity and patronage in the execution of measures of public order. The initiative was left to them in matters concerning religion. The divan served as a malleable and powerful

weapon, effortlessly bowing to—identifying itself with—
French interests, an indigenous magistrature grafted onto the
foreign power, a middle term between the hatred of the conquered and the mistrust of the conquerors.[49]

That description of the limits of the ulema of Cairo's autonomy is corroborated by al-Jabarti, who observed that the sheikhs
of the divan were hostages of the French.[50]

The system of indirect rule that Bonaparte set in place in
Egypt did not consist, as it did in many other colonial enterprises, of using the upper stratum of the indigenous society to
govern: the general in chief would not rest until he had rid himself of the Mamluks, who in his eyes symbolized the pernicious
character of Oriental despotism, or until he had eliminated the
Ottomans in favor of the ulema.[51] He thus sought authorized
representatives, a position occupied in turn or simultaneously
by the Ottomans, the ulema, the Copts, or the *shaykh al-balad*.
The effect of that operation to eradicate the despotic upper stratum was to promote intermediate categories, which supposedly
more faithfully expressed the common people's needs and concerns.[52] In that sense, the ambiguities of indirect rule in Egypt
anticipated the conflicts of French colonizers elsewhere (Algeria, sub-Saharan Africa), who were always torn between two
contradictory imperatives: to govern at the lowest cost and to
find legitimate representatives for the masses.

In the proclamation of 30 June 1798, printed aboard the *Ori-
ent*, Bonaparte told his soldiers: "You will find different practices from those of Europe. You must accustom yourselves to
them. The peoples among whom we are going treat women dif-
ferently than we do."[53]

If we were to take this passage literally, we might be tempted
to detect, in the clash between the French and the Egyptians, the
shock of two cultures fundamentally alien to each other. Similarly, in the following declaration, we may have the sense that
the goal is to divide and conquer, so that the debate will take
place only between the French army and the Mamluks.

The Turks had to be shown the handful of Circassians, the new circumcised, who had been enthroned in Egypt in defiance of Muhammad's successor; the Arabs had to be reminded of the ancient glory of the caliphs and their power over the children of Omar; the Copts, the Greeks, and the Jews had to be given a glimpse of gold and commerce, of the new outlets, and of an industry exempt from harassment; and everyone in general had to be inspired with hatred and contempt for their oppressors.[54]

In reality, nothing would be more misleading than to see the French assessment of certain local customs, or their way of pitting certain segments of Egyptian society against one another, as a notion inspired by cultural relativism or a classic policy of divide and conquer. In contrast to previous colonial enterprises, placed under the aegis of evangelization and mercantilism, the Egyptian expedition introduced a fundamentally new element. The French maintained that the subjection of Egyptian women and the practice of "blood price" were "barbarous" customs not because they were radically other and, in that respect, inassimilable, but because they bore the mark of despotism, fanaticism, and archaism. The splintering of the social body into different segments would thus make it possible to separate the healthy elements from those that were corrupt and to make up for the developmental delays Egyptian society had experienced. By eliminating the despotic stratum, whether Mamluk or Ottoman, the French seemed to have found the means for restoring the natural law that lay within the people and for regenerating the Egyptians. To paraphrase Rousseau, the French came close to claiming that the Egyptian people were fundamentally good and that they had been rendered wicked by the Mamluks. In that sense, the Egyptian expedition was truly the product of Enlightenment philosophy, that is, a philosophy of progress and development. It anticipated a new era of colonization, no longer founded on trade but on the rational organization of production. With the landing of the French expeditionary corps in Alexandria, it was modernity that invaded French colonial policy.

French Multiculturalism
in Algeria

The proper policy may always require that, in secondary jobs,
we have Arabs administered by Arabs, leaving the high
leadership to the French commanders of the provinces and
subdivisions.
—Marshal Thomas-Robert Bugeaud, 17 September 1844

I wanted to tell him [Bory de Saint-Vincent] that, in the end, the
ethnographer Enfantin was less interested in the facial shapes,
skulls, hair, calves, and buttocks of the native races than in the
policy, government, and colonization of Algeria.
—Prosper Enfantin, letter to Arlès, 20 March 1841

The second colonial enterprise conducted after the French
Revolution, the conquest and occupation of Algeria, was
a consolidation phase in nineteenth-century French expansionism. The colonization of Algeria is of particular interest
for the anthropologist striving to evaluate the place reserved for
alien cultures in the French administration system. Through
the Arab Bureaux, a major aspect of French multiculturalism
emerged and was then propagated to the colonies of sub-Saharan Africa, Madagascar, and Indochina. Within that nativist institution, a method for linking knowledge to action was set in

place; that method gave a particular shape both to the oversight of the conquered populations and to the intellectual space within which French ethnology is currently deployed. It was through what I call "assimilative regeneration" that the relativism inherent in ethnology was able to be reconciled with republican secularism.

The conquest and colonization of Algeria, though situated within a context totally different from the Egyptian expedition, displays numerous similarities with the colonial enterprise conducted under the Directory. First and foremost, when the French landed in Algiers in 1830, they saw things through the lenses of Bonaparte and his army. As Tocqueville noted, the soldiers of Charles X, who were about to face Turkish foot soldiers, expected to find before them a cavalry similar to that of the Mamluks.[1] The same was true of Louis de Bourmont's proclamation to his soldiers: like Bonaparte's, it was drafted with the aid of an Orientalist, in this case Sylvestre de Sacy, and implicitly referred to the Egyptian expedition:

Soldiers! The civilized nations of the two worlds have their eyes on you. Their good wishes accompany you. The cause of France is the cause of humanity; show yourselves worthy of your noble mission; let no excesses tarnish the brilliance of your good deeds. Terrible in combat, be just and humane after the victory; your self-interest as much as your duty commands it. Too long oppressed by a greedy and cruel militia, the Arab will see us as liberators. He will implore our alliance. Reassured by your good faith, he will bring the products of his soil into our camps. In thus making the war less long and less bloody, you will fulfill the wishes of a sovereign as loath to spill the blood of his subjects as he is jealous of the honor of France.[2]

Just as Bonaparte wished to liberate the Egyptians from the yoke of the Mamluks, Bourmont wanted to liberate the Arabs from the oppression that the Turkish militia had imposed on them. It was thus the theory of the two races—Egyptians and

Mamluks, Arabs and Ottomans—and the minority policy it assumed (regarding the Jews, Moors, and Kouloughli) that continually informed the intellectual climate surrounding the conquest of Algeria. The predominance of that racial schema can undoubtedly be explained in part by the power of the inertia of certain ideas, but also by the presence within the French army of veterans of the Egyptian expedition.

That residual effect of the Egyptian expedition model, reactivated by the experience of the Saint-Simonians on the banks of the Nile,[3] was not confined to the period of the landing but continued to inform the approach of the conquerors, Thomas-Robert Bugeaud in particular. Although a monarchist, he was clearly inspired by the revolutionary theme of regeneration in his relations with Abd el-Kader, and especially in his conclusion of the 1837 Tafna treaty with the emir, a treaty that constituted the true beginnings of a French nativist policy in Algeria. Even the *Exploration scientifique de l'Algérie* (Scientific exploration of Algeria), that monument of erudition, was conceived on the model of *Description de l'Egypte.*[4]

That continuity of the French colonial project was undoubtedly greatly indebted to the familial and intellectual ties uniting Bonaparte and Napoleon III: the very concept of "Arab kingdom" owes a great deal to the first emperor's ideas about the East and about the administration of the conquered provinces.[5] But, apart from the fact that French nativism cannot be reduced to these two individuals, we should not gloss over the profound differences between the expedition conducted on the banks of the Nile and the Algerian enterprise. Even apart from its duration—more than one hundred and thirty years, compared to three years for the Egyptian expedition—the conquest and colonization of Algeria belonged to a new historical and intellectual context. The "republicanism" and secularism of the Egyptian expedition stand in opposition to the monarchism and Catholicism of the conquest of Algeria. Although Bourmont, in his proposal for a capitulation agreement, claimed to respect the property, customs, and religion of the Algerians, he allowed churches to be built on the site of mosques.[6] Similarly, although Bugeaud set in place a policy of great chiefs reminiscent of the policy of notables initiated by Bonaparte in Egypt, Bugeaud's policy owed more to the principles of a system of landed aristocracy than to a desire for "direct contact," that is, an interest in establishing ties with the Arab masses. Because Algeria became a settlement colony, a series of problems—the delimitation of civil and military territories, relations between Algerians and Europeans, the administration of real property, and so on—that had not been raised in Egypt had to be addressed.

In certain respects, the conquest and colonization of Algeria were linked more to the other European settlement colonies than to a military and scientific expedition conducted under the aegis of triumphant reason. And there was another difference: the nature of the societies in question, in particular, their respective rural areas. There was an enormous contrast between the peasant character of the rural Egyptian areas and the segmentary nature of the Algerian countryside, and one might be tempted to explain the difficulties encountered by the French conquerors in Algeria on the basis of that difference.[7] Nevertheless, the importance, in both regions, of the practice of "blood price" (*diyya*), that is, of a segmentary principle, relativizes the force of that contrast.

Algeria in the 1830s

Although nominally constituting a province of the Ottoman Empire before the French conquest, the regency of Algiers was a semiautonomous military and segmentary state.[8] At the head of the state stood the dey who, in principle, was elected by a high council (divan) comprising sixty officers and high officials but, in fact, was placed under the strict control of the militia of Turkish janissaries (*odjak*), which numbered close to fifteen thousand men. Gravitating to the upper reaches of the state peopled by Ottomans were the Kouloughli, métis descended from Turkish men and autochthonous women; court Jews, whose economic role was considerable; and Moors, members of a middle class descended from Andalusians who had been driven from Spain.

The dey effectively controlled only the territory of the "Prince's Home" (*dar es-Soltan*), that is, the environs of Algiers and the Mitidja plain. Both regions were administered by an Arab aga and four Turkish kaids. The rest of the regency was divided into three provinces (*beylik*): Medea, Oran, and Constantine. These provinces were administered by the beys, the militiamen of the *odjak*, and by the so-called *makhzen*, tribes that, in exchange for certain privileges, collected taxes from the subjugated groups. The *beylik* were themselves divided into a certain number of cantons (*watan*) governed by Turkish kaids. Every canton itself comprised several tribes commanded by autochthonous sheikhs.

This hierarchical organization thus combined the features of a direct rule system at the level of the kaids and an indirect rule system at the lower echelons. But, beyond that segmentary isonomy, there were also factors of inequality. Not all tribes had the same weight: some were semiautonomous, whereas others, such as the Saharan tribes, were directly dependent on the dey.

It was within that structure that the collection of taxes from the masses (*raïa*) occurred.[9] Not all taxes, a large part of which were collected by the royal columns (*mehalla*), reached the central power.[10] At every level, part of them were held back by those to whom they were farmed out, and their redistribution fed a political system based on personal allegiance.

Parallel to that political organization was a dual judicial system. The Turks were governed by Hanefite law, while the autochthonous peoples fell under Malekite law. That network included a mufti and a qadi, who applied the law and the Shari'a.[11]

Matters were rarely brought to court by private individuals, especially outside the cities. Murders and assaults were generally settled by physical or financial compensation (*diyya*), because family members invoked the right to private vengeance (*rebka, thamgert*) against the guilty party or a member of his family.[12]

This rapid overview would be incomplete if I omitted to mention the role of the marabouts, and especially the religious brotherhoods, as a force of opposition to Turkish rule. It was from the anti-Turkish brotherhoods that Abd el-Kader emerged—a person with whom the French would clash when they tried to extend their domination to Algeria as a whole. Although Abd el-Kader's glory days were during the limited occupation, let us briefly mention this marabout's actions since, alongside the military-segmentary state, the French were inspired to establish an indirect rule system built on his political organization. Abd el-Kader's organization can thus be seen as a result of the clash with the French. Inasmuch as the French did not wish to occupy Algerian territory as a whole, it became necessary to fill the void left by the collapse of Turkish power and, in that respect, a state built by the emir may have appeared the best means to control from a distance zones that otherwise would have been left to dissidents.

For the four large divisions of the Turkish regency—the *dar es-Soltan* and the three *beylik* of Medea, Constantine, and Oran—Abd el-Kader substituted a hierarchical territorial organization relying on the caliphs, the agas, the kaids, and the sheikhs. All these dignitaries were civil servants paid by the state and chosen from among the religious cadres. Unlike under the regency, the Islamic dimension took precedence in Abd el-Kader's state. In particular, contrary to the Turkish tax system, the tax system created by the emir established a strict equality among all Muslims.[13] At the judicial level, the punishment of crimes fell to the *makhzen* chiefs, whereas state and private affairs were under the jurisdiction of the tribal qadis.

The coexistence of Abd el-Kader's state and the French-occupied zone established a first division of Algeria. The different modes of division between civil and military territories followed from that first division, which thus opened the way for a nativist policy resting on ethnology. It was almost exclusively through the Arab Bureaux, whose most famous incarnation was the SAS (Sections administratives spécialisées), that this policy was carried out.[14]

The Arab Bureaux: Indirect Assimilation and Separate Development

The creation of the Arab Bureaux, which was the mark of French nativist policy in Algeria, was driven by several contradictory ideas, though in the end those ideas all had a common conceptual base.

Two main conceptions were at the root of the Arab Bureaux operations: that of Bugeaud and that of the Saint-Simonian officers. Bugeaud was an ardent supporter of the "reign of the saber" and military colonization; he also favored a regime of indirect administration that left the management of the military territories in the hands of the traditional headmen.

That legitimist conception, based on an alliance or even a complicity between the French military, often of aristocratic origin, and indigenous notables, stood in opposition to a republican and Saint-Simonian conception that emphasized direct rule.[15] One might think that these two conceptions—indirect administration and direct rule—corresponded to the two ideas driving French colonization: assimilation and association. In reality, however, the ideas of assimilation and association were equally present in both positions. Let us therefore place two quotations side by side: the first, from Bugeaud, is that of an ardent representative of indirect administration; the second, from Ismaël Urbain, is that of a Saint-Simonian, who, for a time, favored direct rule and later became the inspiration for Napoleon III's "Arab kingdom" policy.

In this respect, the conquest of Algeria can be distinguished from the conquests that have sometimes occurred in Europe. There, when a conquered province was held, no one had the pretension of introducing a new people into it; no one wanted to take part of the lands and give them to foreign families who differed in their mores and religion. . . . We always presented ourselves to them as more just and more capable of governing than their former masters; we promised to treat them as if they were children of France, *we gave them formal assurance that we would preserve their laws, their property, their religions, their customs, etc.* We have made the tribes of Algeria feel our might and our power; now we must let them know our goodness and justice and make them prefer our government to that of the Turks and that of Abd el-Kader. We may then hope, first, to see them tolerate our domination, and later, over time, we may accustom them *to identify themselves with us, so as to form one and the same people under the paternal government of the king of the French people.*[16]

European colonization will be gradual, that is, slow and painful. As we wait for our colons to be numerous enough to develop the land, shall we let Arab society live beside us, without taking the trouble to concern ourselves with it, to fulfill our role as civilizers? . . . The administration ought to be inspired by the Turkish regime, which is much more simple than one imagines. . . . Let us administer the tribes through the Arab Bureaux, using the native kaids as intermediaries. The local aristocracy will henceforth have purely honorific titles. Later, the Arab tribe will be able to stand beside the French commune and even to *blend into it. Then we will have a true Franco-Arab association. Association will pave the way for fusion. To bring about that fusion there is one privileged method: the conclusion of mixed marriages.*[17]

Regardless of properly Saint-Simonian terms such as *association*, the same idea can be found in both Bugeaud and Urbain, that of a fusion between the Arab and the French peoples. Without tracing the genealogy of that notion back to ancien régime debates concerning the theme of the war between the races, and especially, to the republican doctrine of assimilation (Mably), let us observe that this problem of fusion is not inconsistent with the two driving ideas behind the Arab Bureaux: the raciology of North Africa and indirect rule.

The French colonizers' apprehension of the Algerian populations was based on a series of reductive moves directed at ethnicity, the Arab/Berber opposition being merely one of these.[18] In fact, the process of assimilating or regenerating the autochthonous peoples by the French could be directed at the Arabs, or, when the latter were considered inassimilable because of certain traits—Islam, for example—at other categories of the population.

Therein lies the full ambiguity of French nativist policy, which appears clearly in Napoleon III's so-called Arab kingdom doctrine.

Although the military regime was reestablished in 1851, the Second Empire defended the ideas of assimilation until 1858.[19] It was only in 1860 that Napoleon III began once more to grant a preeminent place to the Arab Bureaux and to define his doctrine of an Arab kingdom. That doctrine was officially formulated in the letter the emperor sent to Marshal Pélissier in 1861, a letter closely inspired, as Marcel Emerit has shown, by Urbain's *Indigènes et immigrants* (Natives and immigrants).[20] In that letter, Napoleon III declared that Algeria was not an ordinary colony but an "Arab kingdom." In that territory, it was not a project of colonization that was to be carried out but a project of government. And whereas colonization fell under the jurisdiction of the Senate, government was dependent on the emperor. Algeria was thus part of the crown's special domain and the Algerians were the emperor's subjects. Napoleon III maintained that the native Algerians conquered by France would not be oppressed and despoiled; on the contrary, he intended to protect and civilize them. That policy of "redemption," to use a term borrowed from Urbain, was formally reasserted at the reception the emperor gave in Compiègne in 1862 in honor of several Arab headmen.[21] At that reception, Napoleon III reaffirmed the primacy of military authority, objected to the plundering of Algerian lands, and proclaimed equality between the natives and the Europeans.

That pro-native attitude was sanctified with the senatus consultum of 1863, which recognized tribal lands and delimited their territories. At the same time, however, individual ownership of land by tribal members was set in place and a reform of the douars and *djemaa* (village assemblies), modeled on the organization of French communes, was undertaken.

The contradictions of Napoleon III's pro-native policy appear clearly in the decisions made during his trip to Algeria in 1865. During that trip, the emperor decided to partition the country under the authority of the Arab Bureaux in order to prevent the disintegration of traditional society and to civilize the indigenous people through slow assimilation. Inspired by Urbain's *Gouvernement des tribus* (Government of the tribes), Napoleon III distinguished three stages within that assimilation process. During the "Arab" stage, the traditional administrative and social arrangements, as well as the headmen invested with power, were to be kept in place. The second stage was to mark the beginnings of French influence and the phasing out of the headmen in favor of the *djemaa*. During the third stage, the transformed tribe was to smoothly take its place beside the French commune and to fall under the same civil authority. Within that system of partition, all tribes were once more placed within military territories, and the Arab Bureaux were to confine themselves to providing information to the colonial authorities, without getting involved in the local administration, which was entrusted to the tribal heads. Hence Napoleon III and his advisers rallied behind the watchword of slow assimilation of the native peoples under the military's protection, that is, behind the principle of indirect rule. They nevertheless understood that assimilation in terms of the theory of races, since the relationship between the Arabs and the French was considered analogous to that between the Gauls and the Romans.[22]

The measures taken after the emperor's trip only served to confirm the uncertainties of the "Arab kingdom" doctrine, which, even while promoting assimilation, maintained the cultural specificity of the native people. Hence, within the context of protecting traditional societies, lands were retroceded to the tribes and protected against creditors. Similarly, limits were set on expropriation for public use and on the areas set aside for forest reserves and for colonization. At the same time, however, the senatus consultum of 1865 declared that the Muslim native was French, that is, it proposed to assimilate him, even while preserving his personal status in the domains of family (polygamy), property, and inheritance.

The "Arab kingdom" policy thus strikingly illustrates the tensions, inconsistencies, and contradictions of the French theory of colonization. At the heart of the idea of assimilation lay an implicit raciological approach; at the same time, a desire to civilize lay concealed within the principle of indirect rule. It is within that framework that we need to resituate the different areas of intervention by the Arab Bureaux on local Algerian societies. Rather than analyze the various aspects of that policy—education, health, agriculture, justice, ethnology—I prefer to examine the two main pillars of the Arab Bureaux's actions: control of the population and assimilative regeneration.[23]

Control of the Population

It was by virtue of their status as conquered peoples, then as French non-citizens, that control of the indigenous people was called for by officers of the Arab Bureaux. Control of the population essentially took two forms: settlement and surveillance.

Settlement

Until 1845, the French conquerors practiced the so-called oil stain policy, whose aim was to increase the surface area of the territory controlled by the French army by gradually driving back the native population. Bugeaud and the officers of the Arab Bureaux opposed that policy, which, in their view, was contrary to the well-understood interests of the colons. They believed it was preferable to let the native populations live among the Europeans, so that the latter could use their labor power. The new organization, set in place between 1845 and 1863, was called "cantonment" or "contraction."[24] It consisted of placing the seminomadic populations, who usually lived in tents, in among the European settlements. Several methods were used to fix these populations: on one hand, the Arab Bureaux organized the native populations into villages and obliged them to build houses; on the other, they delimited and registered the lands necessary to the tribes, and granted the rest to the Europeans. In fixing the native populations in the vicinity of the colons, French officers attempted to exert effective control over them, by seizing their property if necessary. Distributing plows to the native headmen and developing arboriculture had the same aim: by increasing yields, plow farming promoted attachment to the soil; and the tree plantations rooted the peasants to their land. Hence the settlement of the Algerian populations was inseparable from the close surveillance that the Arab Bureaux intended to practice on them.

Surveillance

It is within the context of the partition of Algerian territory into two major regions, the Tel and the Sahara, a partition that is itself open to a racial interpretation, that we need to resituate the agenda of overseeing the native population. The French quickly concluded that they had only to control the granaries of the Tel, that is, of northern Algeria, to keep under their domination tribes from the south, who came once a year to get fresh supplies from their northern neighbors.[25] Surveillance through control of access to the food supply was only one aspect of a system embracing economic life as a whole. Rationalizing the population's way of life entailed policies as diverse as standardizing weights and measures, introducing French currency, policing roads and markets, recording economic fluctuations, and inventorying agricultural, hydraulic, and mining resources.

Establishing a system for overseeing the lives of the native peoples based on the development of a statistical apparatus made it possible not only to gauge public opinion but also to assure the Algerians' prosperity, which would guarantee the colony's security. Thanks to good harvests, the native people were supposed to forget the trauma of colonial conquest. Nevertheless, that surveillance of the population was not limited to the economic sphere: it also concerned public health, the justice system, chieftaincies, and religious brotherhoods.

In the medical sphere, a detachment of health officers made it possible not only to offer care to the population but also to collect information that lay beyond the administrators' purview.[26] In the justice system, the French intended to restore the repressive apparatus of the Turkish regency and of Abd el-Kader's state, an apparatus that had collapsed with the invasion of the French armies. The Arab Bureaux thus set in place what they called *Hukm el-Makhzen* (the law of the *makhzen*), which had jurisdiction over political and criminal justice. In that system, the native headmen, under the control of the Arab Bureaux, had the right to impose fines, which unfailingly produced a high proportion of arbitrary judgments and a rise in the number of penalties. The kaids, under the authority of the French military, were charged with prosecuting and preventing crime. Above them were the qadis, both judges and notaries, who held positions at the tribal level and on the *medjles*, councils that, under the authority of the Arab Bureaux, were composed of several qadis responsible for examining defendants and hearing appeals.[27]

In 1854, under the Second Empire, the new organization that had been established granted a larger role to indirect rule and made the indigenous justice system totally independent of French tribunals.[28] The new structure determined the rules to be followed in appointing the judicial staff and defined the hierarchy of responsibilities and their territorial jurisdictions. Hence the oversight practiced by officers of the Arab Bureaux on the native justice system was strengthened, even though the latter remained autonomous from French justice. That was not the case under the Third Republic, where it was the French judge, and not the qadi, who applied common law.

One of the functions of the native headmen, under the supervision of the Arab Bureaux, was to control crimes and misdemeanors. In addition to that judicial function, the local chiefs received a whole series of new powers within the new administrative organization set in place by the French after 1830. That organization, modeled on Abd el-Kader's state, was based on the "circle," which called together a group of tribes whose heads were under the orders of a single high commander. Corresponding to the hierarchy of the military command, then, was a hierarchy of Arab Bureaux, which itself comprised several echelons: circle, subdivision, province, and central echelon. Within that structure, the officers of the Arab Bureaux exercised absolute power over their administrees: in theory, they had the power of life and death over them, though they in fact governed largely through the intermediary of the native headmen.

Every Arab Bureau chief had about fifteen headmen under his orders. These subordinate headmen—caliphs, agas, and kaids—had a very broad spectrum of duties: they kept the peace, assembled the goums (requisitioned convoys),[29] monitored the markets, administered justice, and collected taxes. In theory, that last duty fell within the realm of the Arab Bureau chief. He directed the operations of assessing and collecting the so-called Arab taxes, that is, the *ashur* (tax on cereals) and the *zakat* (tax on cattle), in keeping with the model inspired by Abd el-Kader's state. In actuality, in most cases it was the kaids who made the assessment and collected the taxes.

Here again there was an ambiguity in French policy, which, while relying on the major indigenous headmen, relentlessly limited or undermined their power. Truly at issue was the principle of "preservation/dissolution," a principle also at work in one last area, that of the religious brotherhoods and education.

The brotherhoods had always served as a force of opposition to those in power, whether that was the Turkish regime or the

French colonial power. Inspired by Enlightenment ideas, the Arab Bureau chiefs continually expressed their distrust or fear of Muslim scholars and teachers, whom they judged to be both ignorant and fanatical.[30] They therefore believed it was necessary to oversee the brotherhoods by registering the religious orders and the Muslim teaching establishments and by keeping a list of their followers and students (tolba).

The French colonial project in Algeria, based on indirect rule, that is, on the strict surveillance and control of the population, or more precisely, of their headmen, required scientifically describing and analyzing native institutions. The pioneering work of Captain E. de Neveu on Algerian brotherhoods belongs entirely to that discipline, as do, in general, the writings of those who have wrongly been called physical anthropologists.[31] Although Jacques Berque, in a masterful article, has detailed the errors contained within the ethnography produced by the officers of the Arab Bureaux, errors he imputes to the absence at the time of an ethnography worthy of the name, I believe it is valid to characterize a large number of the monographs produced by military men as falling within the realm of ethnology.[32] Within that vast body of work, it is appropriate to distinguish between what falls within the realm of intelligence gathering or "social engineering" proper, and what fully belongs to the area of ethnological analysis. At one extreme would be studies with a direct application, such as the organization charts or lists classifying the population by tribe, faction, and subfaction and assigning the name of a leader to each unit so defined.[33] At the other extreme would be fully elaborated works such as those of A. Hanoteau and A. Letourneux on Kabylia, for example.[34] Among the officers of the Arab Bureaux, most of whom were graduates of the Ecole Polytechnique or of the Saint-Cyr military academy, there were both pure practitioners and true intellectuals; and, though a number of their studies are oriented exclusively toward practice, others attest to the preoccupations of genuine researchers. As such, some of the latter studies were subsequently put to use by academics, Durkheim in particular.[35] From that perspective, the received wisdom that the Arab Bureau officers' mode of apprehending the native populations privileged the conventional opposition between the Arab and the Berber would have to be corrected.[36] Although it is true that this opposition rapidly invaded the colonial literature, it would be wrong to claim that the military were its chief architects.[37] The colonial Berber vulgate spread among the colons as well as among the administrators, and that was undoubtedly because the military's credo—"assimilative regeneration"—could rely on foundations other than the distinction between the Arab and the Berber.

Assimilative Regeneration

The ambiguity in the doctrine of the Arab Bureaux lay in the fact that their assimilative posture was often accompanied by a polygenist point of view. In the nineteenth century, in fact, the theme of regeneration was linked to polygenism.[38] Under the influence of William Edwards, founder of the Société Ethnologique de Paris, some Saint-Simonians, who were also members of that society—especially Michel Chevalier, the bankers Pereire and Rodrigues, the d'Eichtal brothers, Ismaïl Urbain, and Courtet de l'Isle—as well as Bory de Saint-Vincent, adopted a polygenist point of view, but without accepting all the ideas of the founder of raciology.[39] In addition, polygenism was supported by colonial statistics that pointed out the difference in mortality rates between members of the expeditionary corps and Algerians.[40]

The theory of republicanism, based on the principle of the fusion of the races, presupposed the existence of a plurality of groups. Therein lay the contradiction of assimilative regeneration, a posture that, beyond the Republic's generosity, allowed a marginalized other—the native—to persist. The expression "assimilative regeneration" has the advantage of encompassing diverse phenomena in the plant, animal, and human kingdoms.

It also has the merit of situating the problem of "development" within a global context, by linking two fields of knowledge that, as far as I know, have rarely been associated: raciology and the "takeoff" theory of economics.

Human Regeneration

Contrary to received wisdom, the regeneration of the Algerian race was not conceived solely or even primarily in terms of the initial opposition between the Arabs and the Berbers. In fact, that theme was never the only one to be used in the rehabilitation of the Algerian populations.

Although certain officers of the Arab Bureaux, and, in general, certain members of the colonial staff were in fact Berberophiles, others were Arabophiles or simply uninterested in the question of ethnicity. That does not mean, however, that they were impervious to any principle of classification.[41] What is striking about the colonial texts was the permanence, even the strict structural necessity, of binary oppositions, whether these oppositions resulted from an ethnic reductionism (Arabs versus Berbers) or divided the social sphere in some other way. But whether these distinctions were explicitly ethnic or based on other schemata, it was always in racial terms that the cleavage was conceptualized. Hence the oppositions set up between the barbarians and the civilized, the conquerors and the conquered, and the chiefs and the masses were all conceptualized racially. This can be easily explained if we remember that the theme of "association" dear to the Saint-Simonians informs in great part the modus operandi of French colonization in Algeria, especially in the military territories where the Arab Bureaux were working.

It is no more surprising that the theme of "assimilation," to the extent that it was combined with regeneration and fusion—that is, with the osmosis between two peoples—also relied on the conventional schema of the race struggle. In that respect, the following text by E. Pellissier de Reynaud, member of the Commission scientifique de l'Algérie, chief of the Arab Bureau, and author of *Annales algériennes* (Algerian annals) is altogether revealing:

> At this point, we are left with the task of establishing ourselves among the Arabs, both as rulers and as colons; but should our sovereignty be used simply to place them under the same designation, or, more precisely, under the same government, as the French, or will it forever establish the preeminence of one race over another? The latter system was that of the Arabs in Spain and of the Turks in Greece and everywhere else; serious disadvantages are associated with it, since the Jews are practically the only ones not yet weary of being in a position of humiliating inferiority. The former system was that of the Franks in Gaul; it gave birth to the most compact, the most united nation on the planet—the French nation, in short. It is the system of fusion, the only rational one, the only one that offers lasting results, because it is the only just one. The conquerors who follow it are instruments used by providence to modify human societies, almost always to their advantage. The others are only passing scourges. We must therefore adopt it, as both the most advantageous and the most just.[42]

That schema of the Frankish conquest of Gaul, applied to the French conquest of Algeria, is thus employed by an ardent assimilationist who is also chief of the Arab Bureau, an institution charged with implementing a policy of indirect rule. The doctrine of human regeneration in force in Algeria was thus clearly situated within the framework of the fusion of the races, that is, of intermarriage and interbreeding. At no time was the constitution of a pure Algerian race at issue, unless one believes that Berberophilia represents a policy of racial selection or the preservation of a human type.[43]

That attitude favoring the fusion of the races was taken so far that Pellissier de Reynaud, like other members of the military, even recommended marriage with Muslim Algerian women, and some soldiers put the idea into practice.[44] Although it is impossible to separate a preference for interbreeding from the prac-

tice of "marriage in the fashion of the country" (that is, the taking of common-law native wives), that attitude was part of
a powerful intellectual current somewhat connected to Saint-
Simonian ideas. Enfantin, Urbain, and G. d'Eichtal were truly
obsessed with the union of "East" and "West," which was simultaneously a union of "man" and "woman," "white" and
"black," "reason" and "emotion," and so on.[45] Particularly for
Urbain, a Guianese who had converted to Islam, there was a desire to regenerate the Guianese race. That desire was later transformed into a desire to rehabilitate the Arab race, which did not
rule out an interest in regenerating the West through a union
with the East.[46] The theme of the fusion of the races, which was
also the theme of "infusion," was compatible not only with the
cherished Saint-Simonian principles of association and classification by racial aptitude but also with assimilation.[47] From that
perspective, association corresponded to the juxtaposition of
Arab tribes and European colons within the context of cantonment, a stage preceding the fusion or assimilation of the two
peoples. Association and assimilation, then, were not opposing
principles, but rather different phases of the same process.

In spite of everything, however, regeneration remained an altogether nativist doctrine, because the aim of the Arab Bureau
policy was to rehabilitate the local social and political structures, not simply to replace them with a European colony.

Let us now consider the different fields of application of that
nativist policy, in addition to those that have already been mentioned.

Social and Political Regeneration

First and foremost, it is in the political realm that we can best
grasp the effects of that policy. In the beginning, the privileged
instrument for regenerating the Algerian people was indisputably Abd el-Kader himself, whom the French saw as someone capable of governing in their name and hence of responding
to their desire to practice a policy of so-called limited occupa-

tion.[48] When that policy failed and the French were constrained to rid themselves of Abd el-Kader, Bugeaud set in place an indirect administration modeled on the emirate. Nevertheless, the resulting joint administration of the Arab Bureau officers and of major headmen was constantly threatened by the desire to limit the power of the important families.

Several means were used to achieve that end. First, some of Abd el-Kader's state positions—the caliphates in particular—were abolished and were not filled after 1844. The later dispersion of the major native commands had the same purpose, as did the use of headmen from the *makhzen*, that is, of the auxiliary corps (khojas, *chaouch*, spahis) in the service of the Arab Bureau officers. In the end, the regeneration of Algerian political structures was expressed as an interest in giving—or restoring—a republican form to tribal institutions and thereby reviving the principles of public law hidden within the old Roman, Greek, French, or Christian fount of the Arab/Berber masses.[49] That is why Hanoteau and Letourneux undertook to collect and codify Kabyle customs, particularly the famous *kanun*, which were understood as the true constitutions of these village republics.[50]

Beyond the Berber vulgate, the aim of codifying local customs and of studying and applying the Shari'a was to rehabilitate the native justice system, whether it was administered by chiefs or by the Muslim tribunals, which retained a certain role in controlling ordinary crimes.[51] The Muslim justice system needed to be regenerated,[52] because, in the view of the Arab Bureau officers, it was tainted by a certain number of defects or deficiencies such as fanaticism, ignorance, corruption, arbitrariness, and a correlative disregard for the notions of natural law,[53] public punishment, and the uniformity of penalties.

As during the Egyptian expedition, it was the custom of blood price in particular that shocked the French officers. They deplored the existence of a justice system that was as repressive at the level of principles as it was lax in their application. Hence they urged that the practice be purged or gradually abandoned. As Captain Richard declared, it was necessary to "leave to the people their Muslim law, all the while subjecting it to intelligent oversight in its application, to make way for the necessary incursions of our own law."[54] The officers of the Arab Bureaux were very conscious of the composite character of Algerian societies and, as a result, of the impossibility of abruptly and uniformly applying French legislation to them.[55]

The officers' multiculturalism in legal matters appears to have been the result of their perplexity with legal systems that were both similar to and different from their own. For these soldiers, inspired by Enlightenment ideas, it was therefore important to reform certain aspects of the native justice system without calling into question its foundations, while striving to ultimately bring about a fusion of the two systems.

It was especially on the matter of women's emancipation that these principles were developed. The protofeminist officers of the Arab Bureaux wished to relieve Algerian women of their supposed burdens by preventing forced marriages, by limiting polygamy, and above all, by seeing that Koranic law was applied at the expense of local customs. But that agenda of women's liberation was also driven by self-interested motives, since half the population could thereby be won over to the conquerors' ideas.

The French military's attitude toward slavery was completely different. In Algeria, the slave trade was a marginal phenomenon, since one effect of the French conquest was to divert a large part of the trans-Saharan traffic in slaves toward Morocco, Tunisia, and Tripolitania. In contrast, the problem of captivity as a social status was not insignificant: the number of slaves in existence in the first half of the nineteenth century has been estimated at twenty thousand.[56] Slavery, abolished by the French Revolution in 1794, was reinstated by Bonaparte in 1802. Until 1848, the French therefore accepted it in its colonies, especially Algeria, where the capitulation agreement promulgated by Bourmont stipulated that local customs should be respected.

In the name of the proclaimed nativism of French colonial policy, the Arab Bureau officers showed little interest in improving the fate of a minority of the population, a policy that would have run the risk of undermining the authority of the slave-owning notables, whom they greatly needed to maintain order. Hence there was a limit to the generosity of the regenerative doctrine founded on natural law: the need not to disrupt the existing social order. Nevertheless, some republican officers—Pellissier de Reynaud, for example—openly opposed slavery. Rather than return two runaway slaves to Abd el-Kader, Pellissier preferred to resign his post as chief of the Arab Bureau.[57]

The justice system was related to education, since it was in the schools that the qadis and *tolbas* (scholars) who served as judges and notaries in the tribal zones were trained.[58] The Arab Bureau officers had roughly the same opinion about both areas: for them, Muslim education was a victim of fanaticism and ignorance. To counter the perverse effects of the system, the brotherhoods and *zawiya*, the principal vector of opposition to French occupation, initially had to be watched, their resources controlled and their instructors required to pass exams. During a second phase, enlightened teachers would be trained and would transmit their knowledge to the new generation.[59]

It was in the medersas—that is, in Franco-Arab schools where religious and scientific knowledge was transmitted in both French and Arabic—that the program would by preference be carried out.[60] Through such schools, the French intended to train tolerant Muslim judges and scholars who had adopted French ideas. But certain officers, such as Captain Richard, were opposed to the native schools, which they saw as laboratories for fanaticism, and favored instead French schools, which they believed were better able to assure the fusion of the two races.[61]

Hence the multiculturalism of the Arab Bureaux was caught within a profound contradiction, which I have called assimilative regeneration. Isolate, purify, filter, but to what extent? Everything was a matter of dosage. And, in fact, a whole spectrum of positions toward native practices, from preservation to dissolution, could be found among French officers, based on various moral, philosophical, and political tendencies.

The Regenerated Desert, the Regenerative Desert

For those soldiers avidly in search of the absolute, to the point of being tempted to go over to "the other side" of their culture to better identify with the Native, there lay the possibility of fleeing to the south.[62] The Sahara, nomads, and the mirage of trade with the Sudan had the power to feed the fantasies of the Arab Bureau officers, true conqueror ethnologists.[63] Two aspects can be distinguished in that appeal of the Sahara: the regeneration of the desert and regeneration by the desert.[64]

Once again, the projects for regenerating the desert occurred within the context of Saint-Simonianism. The idea of tapping into and reviving the trans-Saharan commercial routes that had shifted toward Morocco, Tunisia, and Tripolitania as a result of the conquest of Algeria was directly related to the Saint-Simonians' preoccupations, though it was not their concern exclusively. Similarly, the many projects for constructing roads, navigable waterways, and railroads through the Sahara were part of the ideological arsenal of Enfantin and his disciples. But although the French officers wished to increase the number of connections between the Maghreb and tropical Africa, they also wanted to give an economic boost to the Sahara proper. Hence the many drilling and irrigation projects, including a project to create an internal sea, whose aim was to assure the economic development of the oases, and more generally, of Saharan agriculture.

This was to be a regeneration of men as well: the Arab Bureau officers, disappointed by the difficulties of colonization in Algeria and by the resistance of the peasants of the Tel, transferred their hopes to the desert. That space, sparsely populated by nomadic people, reinforced their notions of nobility and independence.[65] Similarly, they dreamed of extending France's domination to the desert by eclipsing Morocco and England and, via the Sahara, wished to connect Senegal, run by Faidherbe, to the Mediterranean.[66]

Faidherbe: A Republican Raciologist

When I think that Mungo Park did not speak Arabic!
—Louis Faidherbe

L ouis Faidherbe is known for the administrative work he accomplished during his tenure as governor of Senegal between 1854 and 1861, and again between 1863 and 1865, and for his bravery while commanding the northern army during the Franco-Prussian war of 1870. Less well known is the fact that he was the real inventor of the notion of "black Africa" and that he came up with an a priori contradictory doctrine resting on both an anthropology of race and on republican assimilation.

Although he occupied many posts in the French colonial empire during his lifetime, it was in Senegal that Faidherbe achieved the most prolonged and significant part of his work as a conqueror, administrator, and ethnologist. We therefore need briefly to mention the situation in that colony before his arrival in 1852 if we are to evaluate the impact his predecessors' actions had on his own work and to understand its originality.[1] It was with Faidherbe that, for the first time in the contemporary era, the idea of the singularity of black (sub-Saharan) Africa in relation to white (north) Africa emerged and that the ethnic specter that continues to inform our representation of Senegambia first made its appearance. In that respect, Faidherbe truly stands as the father of French Africanism.

Senegal before Faidherbe

After centuries of presence on the coast of Senegal thanks to its trading posts in Saint-Louis and Gorée, France did not consider abandoning mercantilism until the early nineteenth century, when, following the loss of Santo Domingo, it introduced a timid policy of agricultural development. In 1817, England returned Senegal, which was merely a string of trading posts, to the French government. At the same time, the British prohibited France from reestablishing the slave trade, where most of the colony's value lay. Limited in its freedom of action, France had only two options left: the legal gum trade and agricultural development. Contrary to the old colonial scheme, where workers (slaves) were transported to where the work was located (plantations in the West Indies or the Americas), the development of the gum trade entailed transporting the work to where the workers were. Two names are associated with these efforts at agricultural development in the early nineteenth century: Julien Schmaltz and Baron Roger.

As in Algeria at the time of the conquest, the acclimation of American (Santo Domingan) plants served as the prevailing model in Senegal. Colonel Schmaltz, fresh from his rich colonial experience, particularly in India, came up with the idea of growing cotton, indigo, and sugar cane as a substitute for the declining gum trade. In addition and more systematically, in 1818 he perfected a four-point colonization plan: the construction of forts along the Senegal River; the acquisition, in the vicinity of these forts, of territorial concessions from the native chiefs; the establishment of a European colony using paid native labor; and the development, within the orbit of that European colony, of a new indigenous peasantry. Schmaltz's plan for colonization failed, and it fell to Baron Roger to resume efforts in agricultural development.

Although relying on a range of cultivated plants more or less analogous to those used by Schmaltz (cotton, indigo), Roger's plan for agricultural development included two original elements: the use of scientific farming methods and the desire to improve the living conditions of the native people. The keystone of this plan to disseminate agricultural innovations was the experimental plot, the best-known example of which was owned by Richard Toll. Overseen by Frenchmen—including the famous François Richard—these plots were veritable schools of agriculture. They used a cohort of employees recruited from among the West Indians and local métis, who were then responsible for training the native people. In distributing selected plants to European settlers, Roger and his team intended to develop a model agriculture, which, by example, would boost indigenous farming.

For Roger, that interest in improving conditions for the native people was not limited to agriculture: he was also the first European to publish a collection of Wolof tales and a grammar of that language, thus displaying a strong tendency toward multiculturalism.[2] In spite of Roger's efforts to spur economic development by relying on the native people, that experiment failed and, in 1831, at the end of his tenure in Senegal, the French government gave up trying to make that colony a new Santo Domingo. The old mercantilist policy centered on the gum trade again took center stage, even though, as was often the case in matters of development, Schmaltz's and Roger's efforts were destined to influence France's later economic policy in Senegal.

In the period between Roger's departure and Faidherbe's assumption of the post of governor of Senegal, a period when a multitude of governors followed one after another, there was, simultaneously, a resumption of the gum trade, a rise in peanut farming, and the propagation of a model of conquest and colonization directly inspired by the Algerian experience.[3]

It was comte de Bouët-Willaumez, corvette captain and governor of Senegal from 1842 to 1844, who was responsible for importing the Algerian model, though it was Faidherbe who implemented it fully. Bouët-Willaumez intended, by imitating what he saw being done in Algeria, to move from "limited occupation" to total domination, particularly on the Senegal River. The gum trade was, in fact, hampered by the residents of the Fouta, who plundered ships, and by the Moors, who collected exorbitant "customs fees." In fact, the gum trade as a whole went into crisis because of the antagonism between the Bordeaux merchants and their métis subcontractors. To end that crisis, Bouët-Willaumez proposed using the methods of "moving columns" and "raids," which had established Bugeaud's might in Algeria, and he even imagined launching steamships on the river. From Algeria, he had also brought spahis, who formed the core of the native cavalry troops; and he encouraged the creation of an "Office of External Affairs" in Senegal, commonly called the "Arab Bureau" at the time.

Bouët-Willaumez's nativism, and his desire to establish an indirect rule system, finally found expression in various projects: the construction of a mosque, the creation of a Muslim tribunal, and the establishment of links between Senegal and Algeria. The main lines of Bouët-Willaumez's program, adopted by the interministerial commission of 1850, were applied by Protet, who governed Senegal from 1850 to 1854, but who, faced with the hostility of French merchants, had to surrender his post to Faidherbe.

Faidherbe before Senegal

Between the glowing tributes and the slanderous insinuations, it is no easy task to establish Faidherbe's biography.[4] Louis Léon César Faidherbe was born into a modest family in Lille in 1818. As a young man, thanks to his aptitude in mathematics, he passed the entrance exam to the Ecole Polytechnique. After graduation, he completed his training in military engineering at the Ecole d'application du génie militaire in Metz and received a first assignment in Algeria in 1844. During the two years spent in that colony, he was upset that he could not participate in the campaigns against Abd el-Kader and Bou Maza and was instead compelled, in his capacity as engineering officer, to build roads and military posts.

Nevertheless, that first encounter with Africa had a major influence on his subsequent career and especially on his colonial ideas. During that time, Faidherbe became an Arabophile and an ardent Islamophile, which did not prevent him from expressing a favorable opinion of certain segments of the European colony. He was utterly contemptuous of the European common people in the cities, just as he despised the workers in the Lille region. Nevertheless, unlike Bugeaud and in conjunction with Christophe Lamorcière, who at the time commanded Place d'Oran, he proclaimed himself an ardent supporter of penetration into Algeria by French businesses. Consumed by ambition and dreaming of glory in battle, he also displayed a pronounced interest in history, linguistics, and ethnology, which impelled him to begin learning Arabic. After his first Algerian experience and a two-year stint in a garrison in the French metropolis, he managed to get an assignment to Guadaloupe in 1848.

When he landed in the West Indies, news of the abolition of slavery had just been announced, and Faidherbe found himself caught in the whirlwind following the emancipation of the plantation slave labor force. Moved by the degradation that black West Indians had endured as a result of slavery, he displayed strong pro-black sentiments and learned Creole. Although the reasons for his departure from Guadeloupe are in dispute and his friendship with Victor Schoelcher open to question, his time in the West Indies must nevertheless be seen as the source of his constant interest in regenerating African blacks.[5]

Before being named to Senegal, Faidherbe was reassigned to Algeria in 1849 for a period of three years. During that second stay, under the orders of Captain Pein, he participated in the construction of the fort of Bou Saada, and it was probably under the influence of his superior that he adopted a circumspect, even openly hostile, attitude toward the possibility of reviving trans-Saharan trade.[6] He also distinguished himself under General Armand de Saint-Arnaud during the Kabylia campaign against Bou Baghla, and had his hour of glory when the road traversing the Djurdjura Mountains was opened.[7] The practical experience Faidherbe acquired in the military domain proper and in engineering was later used to advantage in Senegal. He was inclined to make broad use of the Algerian model of conquest and colonization, to the point of comparing El-Hadj Omar to Abd el-Kader, but he also always took care to distinguish clearly between Senegalese societies and those located north of the Sahara.[8]

Faidherbe and Senegal: An Ambiguous Ethnology

Although the periods when Faidherbe devoted himself most to scientific work were also those when he was the least active in politics, it can be argued that the founder of modern Senegal always defined himself as an ethnologist, as that term was understood in the second half of the nineteenth century. Ethnology at the time was a raciology inseparable from the persistent question of the origins of the different human groups. Faidherbe's ethnological vocation, closely linked to his multiculturalism, comes through clearly in a letter he sent to Jomard, president of the Société de géographie, soon after his arrival in Senegal.[9] In that letter, he demonstrates a desire to "make . . . a few inroads into the geography and ethnology of northern Africa," and expresses, as the principal motivation for his request to be assigned to Senegal, the desire to pursue the history and geography of that region.

As soon as he assumed his post in Saint-Louis as captain of engineering, Faidherbe began to learn Wolof. He traveled through various regions of Senegal, particularly the area around the Senegal River, and thus put into practice his program of geographical, historical, and ethnological investigation. His own fieldwork was of limited scope, however, since he collected most of his information in Saint-Louis, from informants far removed from their native regions or through interpreters who had an urban and globalizing vision of Senegalese societies. To those surveys, he added secondhand information provided by his French collaborators.[10] The sparseness of the firsthand information Faidherbe collected should not obscure the scope of his ethnological project, which went well beyond the clichés usually seen in the scientific works of colonial administrators. Although he often took data collected by others, Faidherbe significantly reworked the material, giving it an original form which, even today, has left its mark on the history and ethnology of Sudano-Saharan West Africa.[11]

In the first place, he can be credited for his subtle approach to Senegalese political organizations. Faidherbe was, of course, not the first to describe the Moorish emirates and the elective monarchies of the Fouta, Walo, Cayor, and Wolof: he had an entire tradition of analyzing Senegalese societies behind him, a tradition marked by the names of illustrious predecessors—especially Jean-Baptiste Labat, Gaspard-Théodore Mollien, Anne Raffenel, David Boilat, Carrère, and Holle—whose works he devoured upon his arrival in Senegal. The originality of his work appears fully in the subtlety of his analyses and the distance he took from prior studies.[12] It was on the subject of the Moorish emirates that Faidherbe exercised all his talents as an ethnographer: he brilliantly demonstrated that the relations among the warrior tribes (*hassan*), the dependent tribes (*zenaga*), and the Maraboutic tribes were hierarchical and not contiguous ethnic relations as in Algeria. He also showed that the Marabouts, who were both Muslim religious and Berber speakers, constituted a hybrid social category. He did not allow himself to grant credence to the origin myths justifying that "anomaly" and vainly sought a satisfying explanation for the phenomenon.[13] That early interest in mixed forms can be seen as the beginnings of what would become in his writings a true obsession with *métissage*. This was also the beginning of the logical impasse within which his raciology remained confined.

Faidherbe's study of Moorish political organization therefore represented a valuable contribution to the knowledge of Senegambia in general, and as such it continues to be used by researchers even today. Conversely, another aspect of his work is more questionable, that related to his raciological perspective, which consisted of "downgrading" and "de-statizing" the societies of the region. The political definition of African societies, particularly the coastal societies which were the first to be observed, has always been a stumbling block for anthropology. Whereas the first travelers or compilers such as Labat willingly granted the status of chieftaincy or kingdom to the political organizations they discovered, their successors, especially Faidherbe, denigrated those same societies by refusing to see the "sheikhs" and "servants" they encountered as kings and ministers. Faidherbe's reduction of those societies to the nonpolitical can be linked to his racialization of them. Indeed, the governor of Senegal based his approach to Senegambian societies on a hierarchical grid of multicolored populations.

Faidherbe's Raciology

Faidherbe's raciology, shaped by polygenism, was organized in terms of a tricolor hierarchy: it distinguished among the white race, the red race, and the black race, with each race or group of races itself comprising several subdivisions.

The white race, which included the Europeans, the Arabs, and the Berbers, was the superior race. In *Le Zénaga des tribus sénégalaises* (The Zenega of the Senegalese tribes), published in 1877, Faidherbe adopted a very firm position on the matter: "North of the Sahara is the white man, active, industrious, and tenacious, who struggles against nature and often makes it bend to his laws; south of the Sahara is the black man, who submits to nature like a slave; the black man, against whom the civilized peoples have committed many injustices; the black man, naturally good, with an intelligence comparable to many of the white races, but who, lacking character, that is, might, will, foresight, and perseverance, will always be at the mercy of the races better endowed in that respect with whom he will find himself in contact."[14]

According to him, within the white race of Africa, there was reason to distinguish between the Arabs and the Berbers. It would not be unwarranted to see Faidherbe as a Berberophile, especially in his late work, the result of a third and last assignment to Algeria and of a trip to Egypt intended to corroborate his hypotheses on the origin of the "white" and "red" populations of northern Africa. His Berberophilia, which relied on the imputation of certain cultural traits to that population group—the absence of polygamy, the advantageous status of women, and a republican form of government—was nevertheless nuanced by the observation that this population had intermarried with the Arabs.[15] The result was a "degenerate race," which, in the governor of Senegal's view, was hardly better than the Arabs.[16]

Although during his stay in Algeria Faidherbe expressed a positive view of the Arabs, comparing them advantageously to "common whites," he did not have words harsh enough for those he discovered in the northern Sahara and whom he called "apprehensive and fanatical."[17] Fearing in particular that the Muslim Moors from the right bank of the Senegal River would proselytize among the blacks on the left bank, he opposed that "extension of the influence of the Arab race, the deadly influence of a race that can be called the most wicked, the most inclined to steal and murder, in the world."[18]

The same ambivalence is found regarding the intermediate race between the "whites" and the "blacks," that is, the race of the "red" Fulani.[19] Faidherbe always felt a special fondness for and fascination with the Fulani, whom he deeply appreciated for the delicacy of their features, their smooth hair, and the pleasantness of their language.[20] He linked that last characteristic to the particular conformation of the Fulanis' mouths (orthognathous), a conformation he contrasted to that of the Malinké (prognathous), who, for that reason, spoke a much "harsher" language.[21]

Adopting the hypotheses current at the time, the governor of Senegal, in certain of his writings, imputed to the Fulani an Egyptian or Eastern origin, emphasizing their resemblance to the human figures represented on Egyptian monuments and on the fact that they too possessed zebu. Conversely, in other passages of his work, he classified their language within the linguistic group now called "West Atlantic" (Fulani, Wolof, Serer), and the Fulani within the "black race."[22] Faidherbe found himself at the confluence of two classification systems; and in linguistic matters, he acted like a true precursor of modern Africanist linguists.[23]

Although observing that the Fulani race is rarely found in its pure state as herders, Faidherbe discerned among them innate bellicose and conquering aptitudes that impelled them to found empires and to subjugate the "Negro races." In some sense, however, it was when they intermarried with blacks that the essence of the Fulani race was realized, and, according to him, it was the founding of a Tukulör empire that must be seen as the most conclusive result of that interbreeding.[24] *Métissage* made the Fulani "ardent propagators of Islamism" and the "founders of empires," which for Faidherbe represented both progress and a threat. If the building of African states and empires was largely the result of a raciological history, mirroring what had occurred in Europe after the Celtic, Germanic, and Slavic invasions, the development of those states once they had been constituted was a function of clashes between different groups of métis.[25] Hence, in reference to Fouta Toro, Faidherbe attributed the Maraboutic revolution of "Abd Ould Kader in the eighteenth century to the conflict pitting the Torodo [the product of interbreeding between Wolofs and Fulani] against the Délianké [the result of intermarriages between Malinké and Fulani]."[26] Although he was led to see the Fulani as a bellicose and conquering race, he did not go as far as Raffenel, who, during the same period, feared that El-Hadj Omar would invade the Sudan and even threaten the French possessions in North Africa.[27]

The same ambiguity can also be found regarding the black race. Faidherbe had displayed pro-black feelings in Guadeloupe, where he had been moved by the state of degradation among the blacks resulting from slavery. When he arrived in Senegal, he did not transfer that solicitude to the peoples of West Africa.

He distinguished several subgroups within the black race. The 1853 expedition that led him along the coast of Africa to Gabon had predisposed him against the blacks of the coastal societies, whom he saw as savages engaging in anthropophagy and human sacrifice. By comparison, the Sudanese appeared much more civilized to him.[28] Nevertheless, even toward blacks of the savanna, Faidherbe's attitude was not free of paternalism and racism. He asserted on several occasions that the congenital inferiority of blacks could be attributed to the smaller size of their brains.[29] Similarly, he was shocked that the role of Shakespeare's Othello was usually played by a black, which, according to him, distorted the meaning of the play.[30] Nonetheless, his judgment, even concerning the blacks, was not univocal, and though his thinking was encumbered by stereotypes common at the time, that did not prevent him from assigning a special place to the évolués of Saint-Louis society (noncommissioned officers, interpreters, and employees), whom he worked to promote.[31] The governor of Senegal wanted to protect the black race from the exactions of the superior races (Moors and Fulani)—hence his hostility toward trans-Saharan commerce—though he recognized that métissage with these races produced positive results.[32] Hence he established a hierarchy among the Sudanese blacks, based on the degree of métissage between that race and the "white" and "red" races. We have already seen the place the Tukulör occupied in that schema. For Faidherbe, there was no doubt that the Mandingues, and more particularly the Bambaras, held an altogether similar position. The Bambaras "are the most powerful of all and believe themselves superior to the others," and their language "must be taken for the proto-type."[33] They also possessed racial superiority, manifested es-pecially in the trait of a "bony and well-developed nose."[34]

In Faidherbe's program for the struggle against El-Hadj Omar, the Bambaras, who, like other Mandingues, were "farmers, skilled workers, merchants, and warriors," were placed in the forefront, because of their capacity to resist Islam.[35] As he had for the Fu-lani, Faidherbe saw *métissage* as the realization of the essence of the Bambara race; and regarding those living in the Kaarta, he noted that the preeminent place of the royal Massassi dynasty could be explained by the fact that it had intermarried with the Tamahou, blond warriors from Egypt.[36]

In the hierarchy Faidherbe established within the black race, the Serers and Wolofs occupied an intermediate position be-tween the Mandingues and the blacks of the forest of Guinea. Darker than other blacks, they had frizzy hair and pleasant fea-tures. He depicted them as "noble savages," whose indolence and sweet disposition bore the contradictory marks of autoch-thony and of relations with the Europeans.[37]

The Pure Race/*Métissage* Impasse

Faidherbe's ethnology therefore depended on a shape-shifting raciology that constantly oscillated between two closely linked poles: the search for the *Urrasse,* or original race, and the pur-suit of *métissage.* The governor of Senegal, because of his physique and his background in Lille, probably saw himself as the "blond warrior"; and, like Joseph Arthur de Gobineau and Friedrich Nietzsche during the same era, he considered the Nordic race of invaders a driving force in history.[38] Although he was in search of a pure race that had not been contaminated by external elements, he also insisted on the usefulness of mixing. His preoccupations were essentially of a political nature: what mattered to him was to find legitimate representatives with whom he could establish diplomatic relations. Although the indigenous races, like the Wolofs and the Serers, were easy to get along with, it was only the populations spawned by the "whites" and the "reds" who were capable of rising to the level of civilization. His attitude toward "regeneration" was twofold: he wanted, first, to reinvigorate physically the races most advanced at the cultural level; and second, to develop intellectually the races that were physically most vigorous. In his view, then, the principle guiding relations between the races was that of an exchange between physical aptitudes and moral and intellectual qualities.

From that perspective, the acclimation of the white races to sub-Saharan Africa was connected to the physical aspect of regeneration. Faidherbe noted, in "L'avenir du Sahara et du Soudan" (The future of the Sahara and the Sudan) that "the Moors were able to survive at that latitude only by mingling their blood with that of the blacks. When a family is dying out physically and morally, it is through an infusion of the blood of a young and vigorous Negress that it is given strong offspring."[39] Conversely, the burden for the moral and intellectual regeneration of the Negro race rested primarily on the Europeans.[40]

Regarding the métis of Saint-Louis, however, his position was not unambiguous. Although he displayed hostile feelings toward the mulatto traders and favored the Bordeaux merchants, he persistently encouraged "marriage in the fashion of the country" and even practiced it himself, at the risk of attracting the wrath of the Catholic Church.[41] Behind that desire to regenerate the black race with European blood, we may naturally suspect a desire to relieve the monotony in the life of an officer stationed in the colonies.[42] A love affair with a young and beautiful African woman, without the obligations of marriage, was a good way to occupy the time while waiting to return to France and to legally marry a young woman from a good family. But, beyond these trivial preoccupations, a republican principle based on the fusion of the races should be seen at work. That fusion was considered the means to regenerate both the conquering and the conquered race.[43] Aware of the impossibility of making Senegal a settlement colony, Faidherbe undoubtedly placed his hopes on the métis, the only ones, in his view, capable of bearing the rigors of the climate and of demonstrating the organizational abilities necessary to establish a modern economy.[44] For him, building Senegal also required that the state and Islam be transformed.

The State and Islam

That tension between the admiration and the fear of interbreeding can be seen in two areas closely associated in Faidherbe's raciology: the state and Islam. Although his critique of Labat attested to his inclination to denigrate the native political institutions by reducing them to anarchy, his revulsion/fascination toward the states of Senegambia in general, and the empire of El-Hadj Omar in particular, was based on an evolutionist and naturalistic notion of history that was not very different from that defended, for example, by Herbert Spencer during the same era.[45] For the governor of Senegal, the state, in the form of empires, represented both inevitable progress and a necessary evil in the differentiation of social organisms. In *Le Sénégal, la France dans l'Afrique occidentale* (Senegal, France in West Africa), he declared that "civilization has made great progress in the world only after forming vast conquering empires; in their lifetimes, these are true scourges, but soon after, amidst the rubble they have amassed, fortunate consequences of their passage on earth begin to appear. That is because they created possibilities among men that did not exist in the fractious state in which primitive countries found themselves, which made possible material and intellectual exchanges, to the great benefit of progress. It is just such a phase of humanity that we are about to witness in the northwestern region of central Africa."[46] In that sense, the empire of El-Hadj Omar, despite its bands of fanatical *talibé* (disciples), represented an unavoidable stage in the evolution that was to lead to the definitive establishment of France in Senegal and the Sudan.[47] Faidherbe's way of thinking, which was inscribed within a teleology characteristic of the nineteenth century, left the task of state building to particular races. In that "state-centric" account, the final achievement always fell to the blond warriors who, occupying the top of the hierarchy of races, were best able to make history bring forth the seeds it bore within it.

Although Faidherbe wanted the French state to prevail in West Africa at the expense of local potentates, he was opposed to the growing influence of the Catholic Church and its missions. His republican fervor, tempered by nativism, impelled him to curb the ambitions of the Congrégation du Saint-Esprit and to encourage the rise of Islam, or, at the very least, a tepid form of it. Like his view of the state, the governor of Senegal's attitude toward Islam was extremely ambiguous. On one hand, he regarded that religion as a worldview superior to animism and considered its expansion necessary if African societies were to evolve from the state of barbarism to that of civilization. Islam was a moral factor since it prevented the blacks, particularly the warriors (tiédos), from taking to drink, the true reason for their plundering expeditions.[48] That religion also made it possible to acquire the ideas of justice and equality before the law and thereby to pave the way for building the large state entities that, for him, represented the future of West Africa.[49]

Islam, introduced by the conquering races, that is, by the Arabs, the Fulani, and the Berbers, was simultaneously a threat because, as for the Tijaniyya of El-Hadj Omar, it constituted the base of the empires opposing France. Faidherbe thus preferred a tolerant and secularized form of Islam, a form that seemed particularly well represented by the Qadiriyya.[50] In that respect, it is valid to claim that Faidherbe, who stood in the tradition of republican officers who had served in Algeria, was the inventor of a conception that reduced the Muslim civilization of sub-Saharan Africa to an essentially religious dimension.[51]

Faidherbe's Native Policy

Closely connected to republican raciology, Faidherbe's native policy was a mixture of rationalism and pragmatism. The governor of Senegal's republican convictions led him to adopt a rational, clearly defined policy in many areas: urbanism, hygiene, education, the advancement of women, and racial fusion, for example.[52] Conversely, after he arrived in Senegal, he quickly subscribed to the pragmatic ideas of the Bordeaux merchants, the Maurel brothers especially, and became an ardent defender of their interests. Faidherbe's native policy—composed of limited occupation, a protectorate, and indirect rule—largely espoused the ideas of the Saint-Louis traders, especially in the period that saw the decline of the gum trade and the rise of peanut farming.[53]

When he assumed the duties of governor in 1854, two urgent problems had to be resolved: the lifting of the "customs fees" that impeded the gum trade, and the Moors' incursions on the left bank of the Senegal River and exactions by the *tiédos*, which were slowing the development of peanut farming. From that point of view, Faidherbe's role was in the direct line of the French mercantilist tradition in Senegal and, at the same time, was situated in the more innovative context of agricultural development. That is why, though he envisioned an eventual expansion toward the Sudan, his policy remained primarily centered on a very loose control of African political organizations and on the use of techniques that had proved effective in the military territories of Algeria.[54] The specificity of Senegal compared to Algeria, a specificity Faidherbe noted many times, did not prevent him from borrowing a number of Bugeaud's experimental methods, whose efficacy he had been able to assess when he served under him.

It was for the most part at the level of tactics that the captain of engineering turned to his advantage the lessons taken from the Algerian experience. Raids against the Moors and the construction of forts were directly inspired by the example provided by the duc d'Isly, even though, in that area, Bouët-Willaumez stood as the real precursor. The creation of the spahi corps and of the "Senegalese infantry," directly inspired by the "Algerian infantry," moved in a similar direction, as did the use of French officers who had served in Algeria to lead the troops.

The Arab Bureaux were also at the origin of the Office of Political Affairs, which was the true pillar of indirect rule in Senegal. During his various stays in Algeria, Faidherbe had had the opportunity to evaluate the merits of that nativist institution, obtaining information directly usable on the political and military level. Hence he worked to develop the same type of institution as soon as he was named governor.[55]

The use of geographical, historical, and ethnographic expertise for political ends also brings to mind the example of the French north of the Sahara, and, in that respect, the Commission de la Carte de la Sénégambie (Commission for Mapping Senegambia) was merely a pale replica of the Commission Scientifique de l'Algérie.[56] The division of the Walo and the Cayor into circles, each headed by chiefs chosen from the royal lineages who were responsible for collecting taxes, requisitioning contingents, and administering justice, was also based on the Algerian model.[57] Finally, the fragmentation of the Fouta into distinct political entities was reminiscent of Bugeaud's constant preoccupation to dismantle the "great native commands." The imitation of Algeria went so far that, during the ceremony investing native chiefs in Saint-Louis, the chiefs were dressed in burnous made of green embroidered material.[58]

In matters of Islamic policy, the creation of a Muslim tribunal attested to Faidherbe's desire to protect Koranic law from the incursions of French law and to retain a certain role for indigenous justice, at least where marriage and inheritance were concerned. In the area of slavery, like the situation prevailing in Algeria, the governor of Senegal's attitude was once again not entirely unambiguous. Although slavery was once again abolished in the French colonies in 1848, Faidherbe tolerated slave ownership by the native people and in certain circumstances authorized the use of slave labor by the French. His attitude toward the slaves who sought refuge in French enclaves was rather hesitant: though he freed those who had fled hostile political entities, he expelled, as "undesirable vagrants," those whose masters were on good terms with the French.[59]

On the condition of women, the governor of Senegal's ideas were strangely reminiscent of those of the Arab Bureau officers in Algeria, and even those of Bonaparte in Egypt. Like his colleagues in Algeria, Faidherbe worked to relieve the burden on Senegalese women, setting up steam-powered mills in Saint-Louis designed to spare them the toil of grinding millet.[60] But his solicitude toward African women did not extend to the question of polygamy. Although he belatedly expressed concerns about the matter, it does not appear that he attempted to abolish or limit the institution during his assignment in Senegal.[61]

Finally, where agriculture was concerned, the Algerian model was omnipresent. Faidherbe's notions were connected to the old idea of acclimation of tropical American plants and hence to the practice of his predecessors Schmaltz and Roger. Although he placed himself in the service of Bordeaux trading companies, which encouraged the expansion of peanut farming, he also promoted cotton and indigo farming and continued to bring in seedlings from the experimental plots in Algiers and Santo Domingo.[62] As a general rule, like his colleagues in Algeria, the governor of Senegal saw agricultural development, and the prosperity that was supposed to result from it, as guarantors of the security and peace that ought to reign in Senegalese societies.

The examples demonstrating the "influence of the Algerian experience on French policy in Senegal" could be multiplied ad infinitum. It is very true, as R. Pasquier has shown, that Bouët-Willaumez and Faidherbe, two veterans of Algeria, made their mark on the colony of Senegal as governors.[63] Nevertheless, it would be risky to follow Pasquier when he asserts that the instructions from the minister of colonies at the time, given under Faidherbe's influence, "appear to be the result of a hasty parallelism between Senegal and Algeria, shored up by the belief in a common allegiance to Islam and, as a result, overlooking the diversity of Senegalese societies."[64] Faidherbe's doctrine can be defined as that of a pro-black republican opposed to extending the Arab language and civilization to sub-Saharan Africa. In that respect, we can detect in a number of his decisions a certain reluctance to reduce black African societies to their homologues in North Africa. All his ethnographic and linguistic work aimed to demonstrate the specificity of societies of the West African savanna as a whole, compared to those of the Tel and the Sahara, and the profound originality of each of them.[65] Although he deployed the conventional raciological schema opposing the conquerors and the conquered, applying it both to the history of France and to the history of the Maghreb, and although he transposed it, to a certain degree, to the history of sub-Saharan Africa, using Berbers, Arabs, or Fulani as the state-building force, Faidherbe was also among those who contributed the most to ironing out African reality by identifying contiguous ethnic groups on the maps of Senegambia.

His penchant for republican assimilation and for a moderate nativism ought to be linked to his pro-black attitude. Thus, fearing that the recognition of the Muslim legal system's specificity would give free rein to Arabization in Senegalese societies, he hoped that Muslims would turn instead to the French justice system. His desire to control the Marabouts, to secularize Koranic schools, and to create Franco-Muslim schools cannot be explained in any other way. Without going so far as to champion education in African languages, he nevertheless composed a constitution for the Cayor in Wolof.[66] Similarly, the priority he gave to French in the schools, and his refusal, unlike the practice in Algeria, to publish official documents in Arabic, followed from his wish to protect Senegalese societies from North African influences he judged pernicious. His effort to limit Islam exclusively to the religious domain was also part of the same preoccupation.

For Faidherbe, the border between the Arab Muslim world and the black African world was drawn by the Senegal and Niger rivers, and even in the domain of taxation he refused to slavishly copy the Algerian model. Rather than introduce the various "Arab" taxes collected by the French in Algeria, and later, in Mauritania, in 1863 he created a capitation tax in Senegal, thus marking a clear difference in style between colonization in sub-Saharan Africa and that in North Africa.[67]

The Promotion of Sub-Saharan Africa and the "Pioneers of the Sudan"

It was in the interest of regenerating the black Sudano-Sahelian race that Faidherbe undertook to promote sub-Saharan Africa when, after being assigned a third time to Algeria and after commanding the northern army during the Franco-Prussian war of 1870, he began his political career by allying himself with the republican groups supporting Léon Gambetta. The desire to regenerate black African societies was based on the idea that the peoples of Senegal and the Sudan would vegetate in a subsistence economy so long as they remained subject to the exploitation of Muslim merchants from northern Africa.[68] To break Africa out of its stagnation, the region first had to be freed from north African domination, and, in a second phase, means of communication had to be developed to stimulate trade with the outside world.[69]

Faidherbe's dream of the East, fed by the writings of Mungo Park, René Caillié, Oskar Lenz, and Heinrich Barth, which impelled him to extend French influence to Bamako and Tombouctou, also led him to reject the plans for a trans-Saharan connection.[70] Thus, during his stay in Senegal and after his return to France, he continually encouraged and even backed many expeditions to the inland delta of the Niger.

The aim of all these explorations was to open the way for a peaceful takeover of the area, based on alliances with local chiefs, so as to introduce economic development to the region.[71] On the model of the "Arab kingdom," which had defined relations between the French and Abd el-Kader, Faidherbe envisioned acknowledging El-Hadj Omar as king of the Kaarta once victory over that area had been achieved.[72] In any case, exploration was not enough for him: falling victim to his romantic fascination with the Sudan's gold resources, he became involved in the exploitation of gold mines in Bambouk.[73] To control the Sudan, Faidherbe came up with the idea of building a string of trading posts along an axis stretching from Medina to Bafoulabé to Bamako, but, despite his later attempts to take credit, he did not invent the plan to build a railroad between Dakar and the Niger River.[74] That was, in fact, the idea of Brière de l'Isle, governor of Senegal between 1876 and 1881; the plan was presented to Parliament by Jean Jauréguiberry, also a former governor of that colony, and minister of the navy at the time.[75] But though Faidherbe's role was simply to use his prestige and influence to see that the project was realized, the construction of a railway between Senegal and the Niger delta was so completely in keeping with his ideas that he was pleased to see others accomplish what he had not had the audacity to propose himself.

Similarly, the conquest of the Sudan, undertaken by Joseph-Simon Gallieni and Gustave Borgnis-Desbordes, fulfilled his deepest wishes, and the two "pioneers of the Sudan" did not fail to invoke the support of the former governor of Senegal to justify their advance toward the east.[76] Faidherbe thus stands as the true creator of "French West Africa," a group of colonies along an east-west axis, of which Dakar would later become the capital.[77]

Faidherbe's Posterity

The intellectual matrix conceived by Faidherbe to apprehend and master the societies of West Africa was extremely effective; traces of it can be found not only among his immediate successors but also in the works of more recent authors, and even in the relations that the different societies of that region have maintained with one another.

His writings served as a source of inspiration for a whole line of military men and colonial administrators/ethnographers, who simply appropriated his ideas when they did not explicitly acknowledge his influence. The governor of Senegal's closest disciple was indisputably Louis-Gustave Binger, whose works display many similarities to those of his predecessor. Faidherbe published the first study of the young Binger on the Bambara language, selected him as an aide-de-camp, and sent him to Senegal to conduct a study of the Wolof language.[78] He also encouraged Binger to undertake his wide-ranging tour of the Sudan and Ivory Coast, and the book that resulted bore the mark of one of Faidherbe's driving ideas, the exploitation of sub-Saharan Africa by the Maghreb.[79] Similarly, Binger's later works, particularly those devoted to slavery and Islam, contained views very close to those of Faidherbe, who, in general, served as the major source of inspiration for the ethnography and raciology of the inland Niger delta explorer.[80]

It would also not be unwarranted to see Gallieni as a direct descendant of the governor of Senegal. The "race policy" introduced by the commander of the Haut-Fleuve (Senegal)—that is, the notion that "any officer who has succeeded in making an adequately vast ethnographic map of the territories he commands is very close to achieving complete pacification"—owes a great deal to Faidherbe's ideas.[81] Similarly, the idea that, in order to do battle with Muslim empires, the Bambara and the Malinké "animists" of the Sudan had to be pitted against El-Hadj Omar's "fanatical" Tukulör, is directly descended from the Muslim policy defined by the governor of Senegal.[82]

In fact, all the "pioneers of the Sudan," in rallying behind the principles of eastern expansion and of the delimitation of Senegambia, effectively situated themselves within the sphere of influence of Faidherbe's ideas. It is true that Jauréguiberry, during his tenure as governor of Senegal between Faidherbe's terms there, set in place a system of direct rule in opposition to that of his predecessor. But later, when he became minister of the navy, he hastened to follow closely the Sudanese policy of his former colleague.[83]

The influence exerted by the author of *Le Sénégal* on the works of Ponty, Lyautey, Marty, Delafosse, and on the writings of the inventors of "negritude" could be traced ad infinitum, because Faidherbe, as the father of Africanism, served as a model for a long line of colonial administrators/ethnographers, academic ethnologists, and African intellectuals.[84] It was Faidherbe's guiding idea—the radical originality of the black societies of sub-Saharan Africa, compared to their homologues in North Africa—that, since the second half of the nineteenth century, has made its mark not only in the literature but also in the relations that the various societies of that region have established with one another.[85] The major division between "white" Africa and "black" Africa, which has served as an explanatory matrix for all the "racial" conflicts occurring in Senegal, Mauritania, Mali, Niger, and Chad, are, in the last analysis, indebted to his pioneering notions. By driving the Moors back to the right bank of the Senegal River, by protecting the black populations on the left bank, by filtering and extracting the different ethnic types, Faidherbe opened the way for a breakdown in the relations among societies, which has contributed toward the present-day physiognomy of settlement in northwestern Africa. In reality, though he was not the "inventor" of black African societies, in the sense that others before him, the Arab geographers in particular, characterized the countries located in sub-Saharan Africa by the color of their inhabitants' skin (*bilad es-sudan*), he was the first to have given a raciological—that is, a "scientific"— foundation to the specificity of the dark continent. In that respect, his racism, inseparable from his ethnography, was truly "modern," since it was dependent on an "objective" description of the somatic characteristics of the observed populations. Hence the fearsome force of Faidherbe's ideas—in his desire to regenerate Sudano-Sahelian societies, he opened the formidable Pandora's box of tribal wars and border conflicts in that region.[86]

Multiculturalism in France

T he enterprise of "assimilative regeneration" as it operated in the colonies was only the projection of a notion
elaborated in France in the late eighteenth century, a
notion that had its heyday during the Revolution. In metropolitan France, assimilative regeneration was first applied to the
ethnic and religious minorities living on French soil, then to the
various communities of foreign immigrants who joined them.
Essentially, the effect of the republican crucible was to draw a
line between the secular and the religious, the private and the
public. The various Jewish communities in France were the first
to be implicated in that process.[1]

From the Jewish "Nations" of France to the Israelite French

Because of their exclusion and the marginal position they occupied in French society, the Jews fell into the category of ethnic minorities. Even the generic term "Jews" invites confusion,
since, under the ancien régime, the Jews were not a homoge-
neous group having a clear awareness of their unity.[2] Before the
French Revolution, there were simply two communities in
France—the "German nation" and the "Portuguese nation"—
plus the Jews of Comtat Venaissin. These two communities

lived at a great distance from each another and maintained no relationship between them: they had different customs, observed distinct rites, and did not speak the same language. The isolation of these communities from each other was reinforced by the attitude of the ancien régime, which did not recognize the Jews as individuals and agreed to acknowledge their existence only as collectivities. The autonomy of the Portuguese and German "nations" was sanctioned at the legal level by an indirect rule system which, in the name of the "personality of laws," allowed each of the different Jewish communities to administer itself. Hence, mirroring what would be done later in the colonies, the Jewish nations of France were granted autonomous legal institutions and levied their own taxes.

In that case as in many others, awareness of a common identity emerged only in an environment external to the different communities—namely, Paris, where the presence of "Germans" from the east, "Portuguese" from the southwest of France, and former residents of Comtat Venaissin made it possible to transcend the divisions that distinguished the three Jewish nations of France and to subsume them into a single entity.[3] Similarly, the appearance of a religion common to the Jews of France was the consequence of emancipation, which occurred in the course of the Revolution, since, under the ancien régime, religious identity was inseparable from allegiance to the different nations structuring French Judaism. Before 1789, French Judaism was composed only of "discrete" elements, homologous segments that lacked the unity conferred on the Catholics by the Church, for example.

The emancipation of the Jews was the goal of a whole current of thought, espoused by Chrétien Malesherbes among others and particularly well represented by Abbé Grégoire. Grégoire, whose role in the abolition of slavery and the promotion of the Africans is well known, was one of the names attached to the "regeneration" of the Jews. Abbé Grégoire recommended having the Jews of France blend into civil society by making their communities disappear in favor of an assimilation of individuals.[4] That process implied that the Jews would give up everything in their civilization that was not part of the religious sphere. As Abbé Grégoire declared: "One must distinguish in Mosaic law between what lies essentially within the practice of the faith and what pertains only to civil and criminal jurisprudence. Let us grant the Jews full liberty on the first matter and let the rest be subject to national laws."[5] Extracting religion from their overall communitarian practices was not enough, however, to assure the Jews' assimilation; it was also necessary to dissolve their racial homogeneity by proscribing customs, such as the levirate, that led the community to withdraw into itself. It was through mixed marriages and interbreeding that the physical defects of the Jews, which resulted from endogamy, would be regenerated.[6]

Although a fierce supporter of assimilation, Grégoire did not rule out the possibility of having communities that, though standing apart from one another, would all be connected to the commonwealth: "A few provinces in Poland and Russia offer a bizarre mixture of various religions. In close proximity are a Protestant who eats chicken on Friday and a Catholic who eats only eggs. Both drink wine and work on that Friday, next to a Turk who, circumcised like the Jew, abstains from wine and does no work on that day; and this diversity does not disrupt civil harmony."[7] Through that example, Grégoire established the model of what is now called a multicultural society, without troubling himself to test the coherence of that intercommunity life or to verify its compatibility with the structures of a secular Republic. His hesitations express the difficulty of drawing a sharp line between the private and public domains.

During the debate undertaken in the Constituent Assembly that led to the emancipation of the Jews by the National Assembly on 27 September 1791, it was the secular and assimilative dimension of Grégoire's thought that prevailed. In his famous speech to the Constituent Assembly, the duc de Clermont-Tonnerre declared: "One must refuse everything to the Jews as a nation and grant everything to the Jews as individuals;

one must refuse legal protection for the maintenance of the so-called laws of their Jewish corporate body; they must no longer be either a political body or an order within the state; they must be citizens on an individual basis."[8] Similarly, the Jewish religion had to be made to conform to the laws in force, that is, to natural law, since, as Clermont-Tonnerre also said: "Every faith has to prove only one thing, its morality. If any faith commands theft and arson, not only must eligibility be refused to those who profess it, but it must itself be proscribed."[9]

Hence, just as an autonomous entity, the Jews of France, was being constituted as a discrete totality composed of its various nations, that entity was called upon to disappear and give way to the "Israelite French." In a dual movement, the French state produced both a community and a group of individuals, while restricting the religious freedom of citizens out of respect for the laws of the Republic. During the Revolution, Jewish mores and customs were strictly monitored and a number of customs, such as animal sacrifice and the wearing of beards and sidelocks (peot) were prohibited.[10] Similarly, circumcision was harshly combated by Robespierre and his friends, who wanted to eradicate a custom they judged barbarous.[11]

Through the revolutionary process, a distinction was established between realms that people clearly wanted to keep separate, the private and religious on one hand, and the public and political on the other. If we look back at how these two realms were distinguished and at the variants affecting their respective spheres of influence, we see that secularism is a constructed phenomenon, and that, as such, it cannot be considered an absolute principle. It was within the context of that process that the regeneration of the Jews—that is, the constitution of a body of Israelite French citizens—came about under the Directory and the Empire. Nevertheless, that process was not univocal and Napoleonic policy sometimes had the effect of recreating the conditions prevailing under the ancien régime.

When Bonaparte was in Egypt, he was anxious to further the advancement of the Jews. When he became emperor, he set out to bring to fruition the emancipation efforts begun in the revolutionary period and to give the French Israelites new organizational frameworks. In 1807, to complete that reform, Napoleon summoned an assembly of notables, who sent the Jewish community a series of questions on how Jewish customs conformed with civil law.[12] Of these questions, let us mention in particular that pertaining to divorce, which was permitted by Jewish law but banned at the time by the French penal code. The ban on mixed marriages, or, more precisely, on a Jew marrying a Christian, also posed a problem, since physical regeneration was understood as one of the preconditions to assimilation.

The Jews were also asked whether they had an allegiance to the laws of the empire. They were called upon to choose between the obligations of citizenship and those stemming from the religious community, obligations that connected them to Jews in other countries. That question was connected to the status of the rabbinate and the respective place to be granted to civil versus religious jurisdiction in the governance of Jews of the Israelite faith. Finally, the Jews were asked whether usury was inextricably connected to their way of life and whether that reprehensible practice was observed only with respect to Christians or was also in force within their community. More than just a questionnaire, these requests for information addressed to the Jews were a way of testing them and assessing their desire to submit to the civil laws of their country. These methods were again used at the Great Sanhedrin that was convoked by the emperor in 1807.[13] Adopting the distinction between the religious and the political provisions of Judaism, and arguing that the latter had to be abolished, the Jewish notables and the higher civil servants of the Napoleonic state established the Jews' obligation to submit to the laws of the empire and set in place the religious structures that have organized the practice of religion by Israelite French people down to our own time.

The proposed system divided France into a number of synagogues and Israelite consistories, all subject to the authority of a Central Consistory. Within that system, the salaries of rabbis based in the synagogues and in the Central Consistory were fixed but not paid by the state, unlike the salaries of clergy of other faiths. The consistory system, in granting a major place to the state in matters of religious life, gave preeminence to the rabbis in managing the faith; until that time, laypersons had always played a major role in the life of Jewish communities. Paradoxically, because each rite—the French, the German, and the Italian—was assigned a different consistory, the former "nations" of the ancien régime were recreated.[14] By contrast, the term "Jew" was replaced by "Israelite," and Israelites were ordered to adopt legal given and family names. That innovation completed their integration into the French nation.[15]

Thanks to that set of measures, the process of assimilating the Jews to other French citizens was largely underway. Two indicators point to this: first, the disappearance, during the 1870s, of the terms "German" and "Portuguese," though the terms "Ashkenazi" and "Sephardic" were substituted for them; and second, the decline during the same period, observed by Chief Rabbi Isidore, of the practice of circumcision, after that ceremony was moved from the synagogue to the home.[16] All in all, thanks to the Enlightenment, the Revolution, and Napoleon, the Jews of France successfully integrated by becoming Israelites, but they also managed to preserve certain practices, such as circumcision, that were considered barbarous. Did the other "nations" existing on French soil undergo such an effective process of assimilation? Drawing on the studies of specialists on that question, I now attempt to examine the conditions of integration for the other minorities living in France.

The Other "Nations" of France

It was only in the second half of the nineteenth century that "quantity" immigration replaced "quality" immigration, to use G. Mauco's terms.[17] In the eighteenth century, there were few foreigners, and they were for the most part Dutch, Germans,

Italians, and Spaniards who had come to France to work as specialists.[18] As late as 1851, there were only 380,000 foreigners, that is, 1 percent of the population. These foreigners were primarily located in the border regions: Belgians and Dutch in the north, Germans and Swiss in the east, Italians in the southeast, Spaniards in the Pyrenees region. The Dutch-Belgian group by itself represented half the foreign population of the time.[19] Until about 1870, in any case, foreigners were not singled out for any particular classification or exclusion.[20]

It was during the second half of the nineteenth century and the early part of the twentieth that the foreign population increased considerably and that foreigners began to be identified as such, with the establishment of two major institutions to monitor them: the identity card and the Civil Code.[21] During that period, the foreign population grew from 800,000 in 1876 to nearly 1,200,000 in 1911. The neighboring countries of Belgium, Germany, Switzerland, Italy, and Spain accounted for more than 85 percent of that immigration.

Unlike during the ancien régime period, the immigrants were in large part laborers. Between 1910 and 1930, the Italians led the way, followed by the Poles, the Belgians, the Spanish, and the Czechs.[22] Although the Italians were integrated without any great difficulty, the case of the Poles was more sensitive, because of the attitudes of the Polish government and of French employers.[23] The Italians, in fact, would have nothing to do with the "Italian schools"; they took advantage of a 1927 law to become naturalized citizens and often opted for mixed marriages. By contrast, the Poles maintained their specificity by attending Polish courses offered in the public schools or Polish private schools, and by participating in many cultural associations that fostered their sense of identification with their native country.[24] The administration of the Polish community in France by the host society, especially by the mining companies in Nord and Lorraine, thus delayed its integration but ultimately did not prevent it.[25]

Because the Polish immigrants arrived later than the Italians, they did not enjoy the benefits that a first wave of immigrants already living on French soil might have provided them. This fact has led analysts to argue that the Polish population was farther removed from French culture than the Italian immigrants, and hence more difficult to assimilate.[26] Nevertheless, in the end, the result was identical, and second-generation Poles became part of the French melting pot.

The examples could be multiplied ad infinitum to show that the populations judged most resistant to integration because of their cultural remoteness—the Jews of Central Europe, the Armenians, and so on—also assimilated to the French nation.[27]

M. Hovanessian points out that most of the Armenians, who arrived in France in 1922–23, were naturalized in the wake of World War II.[28] Nevertheless, though they integrated in enormous numbers, they did not totally blend into the French political body.[29] Armenian identity was played out over three generations. The first generation encouraged their children to preserve their native language but did not manage to curb the rise of French, which spread by means of the educational system. Until the eve of World War II, the "community" did not feel the antagonisms that may result from dual cultural references; and, until 1966, mixed marriages were rare.

The second generation was truly split between two cultures: it juggled two languages and moved between two worlds. Notable changes occurred only in the third generation: at that stage, Armenian culture became a true "resource" that the Armenians drew on to construct an original identity for themselves. In fact, the newly defined community was shaped less by ethnic values than by memories of genocide, which served as a founding myth for the diaspora communities. As M. Hovanessian observes, "The permanence of identity is built on the memory of exclusion and not on a similarity of mores. . . . The sense of community has taken shape in the group's consistent loyalty, since 1930 in France, to an annual reinvigoration around the date of 24 April 1915."[30]

That analysis can be applied to other ethnic and religious mi-

norities living in the French Hexagon—the Jews especially—
since these different groups all have in common a palette of cultural elements from which they can draw to solidify their identities. In fact, the assimilation of foreigners or outsiders residing
in France has occurred without obstacles so long as the various
institutions set in place to that end—schools, the army, political parties, trade unions, etc.—have done their job properly.[31]
As soon as the integration process begins to weaken, however,
individuals can play on the entire register of identities at their
disposal, either by referring bilaterally to their group identity or
by appealing to an identity farther up the genealogical chain.
Hence communitarianism or ethnicization results less from the
difficulty of assimilating culturally remote groups—the Muslims in particular—than from the impossibility of making the
republican melting pot work at full capacity.

After World War II, the republican model prevailed over
Mauco's ethnicist model within government institutions.[32] It
was therefore decided that integration would occur on an egalitarian basis and not on the principle of ethnic quotas inspired by
the U.S. example and resting on a racial ideology.

It was also during the postwar period that the composition of
the waves of immigration changed markedly, with a rise in the
number of foreigners from Africa (the Maghreb and sub-Saharan
Africa), which by 1982 almost equaled the number of Europeans. Nevertheless, the victory of the principle of republican
assimilation was short-lived since, with the presidency of
Georges Pompidou, an implicitly ethnic/cultural logic was set
in place by the government. But it was particularly with the suspension of legal immigration in 1974 that the French state's individualistic position began to be undermined. The laissez-faire
policy of President Valéry Giscard d'Estaing and Secretary of
Immigration Pierre Dijoud consisted of favoring the long-term
legal residence of foreigners, with a slight advantage given to
those who were ethnically and culturally similar to the French.

In the social, cultural, and religious spheres, the state developed native language courses in the schools and encouraged the

rise of Islamic practices in the factories and housing projects, which made it possible to offer the immigrants' native countries compensation for the suspension of immigration to France. These states were thus given the opportunity to increase control over their populations as, behind a mask of respect for cultural identities, the French government encouraged any workers and families who desired to return home to do so.

The Acclimation of Islam

In 1974, a policy that actually promoted French Islam was set in place, a policy whose effects can now be observed in the flowering of Islamist movements on French soil. In addition to providing Arabic classes in the public schools, the government has worked to ensure the expression of the immigrants' cultural identity by creating television programming,[33] allocating sites for mosques, creating Muslim cemeteries, and purchasing religious books in cooperation with the native countries. That communitarian policy even goes so far as to authorize the payment of salaries to imams, contradicting the principle of separation of Church and state. In reality, the indirect rule of entire sectors of the population has been set in place, mirroring the system attempted during the interwar period with respect to the Italians and the Poles. Always seeking legitimate representatives, the French state and French employers practice a sort of internal colonialism, using leaders who have emerged from the Muslim communities of France to maintain order in factories and workers' hostels. As in the 1920s with the Poles, they hope thereby to offset the pernicious influence of the trade unions and to maintain social order by safeguarding the immigrants' religion.

A policy of *insertion* rather than *integration* was pursued during François Mitterrand's first term (1980–87). Mitterrand strove to keep the immigrants from returning home, to normalize their status, and to support their right to vote, at least in local elections. His second term saw a continuation of the same policy, particularly well represented in the person of Georgina Dufoix, minister of emigration, who preferred a pluricultural perspective that was respectful of difference. Hence, at the initiative of Pierre Joxe, minister of the interior, a Conseil de réflexion sur l'islam en France (CORIF, Council of reflection on Islam in France) was created in 1990. Charles Pasqua, minister of the interior under the second "cohabitation" government in 1993, inaugurated the Institut de Formation des Imams (Institute for the training of imans), and set up the Coordination des Musulmans de France (Coordination committee for the Muslims of France).[34]

The aim of all these measures, and of the formation of a Conseil consultatif des musulmans (Consultation council of Muslims of France) was to create what could be called a "Muslim Church of France," somewhat on the model of the Great Sanhedrin and the Israelite Consistory as conceived by Napoleon.[35] The effort to Gallicize Islam has a long history, which I shall briefly sketch before considering how it has had to confront the particular way that the various groups treat that religion.

The first efforts to acclimate Islam to France go back to 1895 and the idea expressed by Harry Alis, founder of the Comité de l'Afrique française (Committee of French Africa), to establish a mosque in Paris.[36] After many vicissitudes, the plan was realized as a "Muslim Institute" in 1921. It included, in addition to a mosque, a Moorish bath and a craft shop. In the minds of the ruling powers at the time, this undertaking satisfied a threefold concern: to reinforce the cohesion of the colonial empire, to conduct an active Muslim policy, and to demonstrate symbolically the mother country's recognition of the sacrifices of the many Muslims killed in World War I while serving in French uniform. Consistent with the Muslim policy pursued in the French colonies, an effort was made to reinvigorate Islam, to work toward the constitution of a French form of Islam by transforming Algerians into Muslim French, and to establish alliances with the indigenous notables who supported France. Louis Lyautey's speech of 19 October 1922, when the cornerstone of the Muslim Institute was set in place, demonstrates the multiculturalist preoccupations governing its construction and expresses the desire to respect a certain balance between Islam, Catholicism, and republican secularism: "When the minaret you are erecting is built, one more prayer will rise toward the beautiful sky of Ile-de-France, a prayer of which the Catholic towers of Notre-Dame will not be jealous. . . . What those who truly want to serve France in the Islam nations must fully realize is that it is not enough to respect their religion there: they must also respect other religions, beginning with that into which our country was born and grew up. But that respect does not require the slightest abdication of individual freedom of thought."[37]

It was clear what direction Islam would take in establishing itself in France when, in 1957, Si Hamza Boubakeur, a major Francophile notable, was named director of the Institut musulman de la mosquée de Paris. Hamza Boubakeur aptly symbolized a moderate Islam, intended in the first place for the Muslim French, especially the *harkis*. Even though the Institut musulman was financed by the French government, it was unable to make inroads among all Muslims in France, and, during the 1970s, some six hundred Islamic houses of worship were created on French territory.

The Development of Muslim Communities

During that period, there was a dispersal of French Muslims as a whole and, in particular, a very sharp cleavage between Muslims originally from the Maghreb and those from sub-Saharan Africa. In addition, black African Muslims from each country or region tended to identify themselves strongly as separate communities. That was the case for the Soninke of Senegal, Mauritania, and Mali, who had been coming to work in France since the 1960s.[38] At first, the Soninke sent young men to France who stayed only a few years, but, when legal immigration ended, they gradually began to send family members to join them and hence to promote permanent settlement in the host country. That new form of migration led to profound transformations in the very structure of the community and modified its relation to its native country.

Soninke societies were organized into a multitude of politico-religious chieftaincies that did not constitute an ethnic aggregate with a clear awareness of its unity. Migrations occurred and recurred within the framework of village communities with three extremely hierarchical strata: the nobles, the members of castes, and the slaves. The control exerted by the nobles and elders, both within the village and at a distance, over the slaves, caste members, and members of the younger generation, assured order and established a migratory rotation. Within migratory networks, Islam, which was under the control of the Marabouts (*moodine*), was essentially segmentary, since, unlike other populations from Senegal—the Murids, for example—there were no highly structured brotherhoods among the Soninke. With the permanent settlement of members from different Soninke communities in France, and the correlative renunciation of the idea of returning home, a change occurred in the self-awareness of individuals and groups. Although the Soninke had not had a sense of belonging to a social context beyond that of the village or chieftaincy, permanent settlement in the host country led them to acquire an overall consciousness of their place within the Soninke ethnic group. In this case as in many others, it was exteriority that created the homogeneity of the group, which otherwise would have had only an atomized existence.

The creation of the Soninke ethnic group through emigration, a process whereby discrete elements congealed to form an identity, was accompanied by a concomitant transformation in the forms of adherence to Islam. The Soninke shifted from a segmentary Islam under the aegis of the Marabouts to communitarian forms of Islam, which expressed a sense of belonging to an ethnic group. In fact, parallel to an ethnicization of Islam, an

Islamization of the ethnicity occurred. Even as the Soninke ethnic group, that is, a "Soninke citizenry," was being created, there was a leveling of the different social strata, a leveling facilitated by recourse to forms of Islam extending beyond the framework of the hierarchized village communities. Thanks to these new forms (*tabligh*, *wahabiyya*), slaves and caste members could transcend Malekite Islam within prayer communities (*daawa*) and could advance socially. Wahhabism and Sunnism abolished on principle any intermediary between the Muslim and God and, contrary to the Islam of brotherhoods, established strict equality among all believers.[39] But, paradoxically, the use of inclusive forms of Islam did not provide the instruments necessary to establish a community extending beyond the limits of the Soninke ethnic group as it had been produced by emigration. Reformist Islam, based on the conversion, or rather, the re-Islamization of the Soninke, essentially caused community unrest and provided the Soninke with a marker allowing them to distinguish themselves from other Muslims. At no time did a collectivity of French Muslims come into being, and there is still keen antagonism between those whom the Soninke call "Arabs" and themselves. So it was that, when the CORIF was founded in 1990, the black African Muslims joined with French people from the Comoro Islands to found the Fédération des Associations islamiques d'Afrique, des Comores, et des Antilles (FIACA, Federation of Islamic associations of Africa, the Comoro Islands, and the West Indies), which they believed would better represent their aspirations.

Hence the weakening of republican assimilation processes has led to the emergence of Muslim "nations" of France, analogous, in some sense, to the Jewish "nations" of the ancien régime. The development of Islam, in particular of its reformist or fundamentalist forms, is a sign of the permanent establishment of these communities that, in forging a new identity for themselves, thereby create another "home." That solidification of Muslim communities, grafted onto the different forms of

Muslim fundamentalism, corresponds to a rigidification of French identity, or rather, to the shift from a republican to an ethnic conception of the nation.

Toward an Ethnic Conception of the Nation

Throughout this book, I have continually highlighted the racial foundation on which the French notion of assimilation rests. Of course, that conception is founded on a direct relationship between the state and its citizens, on a conjunction between citizenship and nationality, on jus soli, and, recently, on a conception of chosen membership in the national community.[40]

From that standpoint, citizens appear as atoms and there can be no place at all for groups organized into communities. According to republican doctrine, there are no intermediate bodies between the state and the citizens, and it is no accident that it was under the Vichy regime that a conception of the state appeared that interposed a whole set of corporate bodies between the state and the citizens. At the same time, however, the French conception of assimilation coexists with a pluriethnic theory of the national body (Franks/Gallo-Romans); and in many orthodox republican writings, as we saw among the officers of the Arab Bureaux and of the Office of Native Affairs, assimilation presupposes the absorption of one group by another or the mingling of these two groups, including through mixed unions. As soon as the prior existence of these groups is acknowledged, whether the groups are racialized or not, there is nothing to prevent them from being considered minorities that are impossible to absorb.

That is truly the situation in which France finds itself today. The different communities on French soil have engendered, in a kind of reactionary move, a French ethnic group. The French political body—that is, the body constituted by the state and its administrees—appears increasingly to be a conglomerate of communities among which a new social contract must be established. The crisis of political representation proceeds in part from the state's inability to take responsibility for the different communities, in the absence of instruments sensitive enough to register collective demands. The French state, founded on an atomistic conception of its mandate, can settle problems only on an individual basis and must therefore deny any official representation to communities. Nevertheless, it does not fail to name them as such and exercises an indirect style of rule over them.[41] We are witnessing a true crumbling of the political body: the combined existence of the state and of social classes are no longer able to convey the aspirations of social actors.[42]

The crisis of political representation is a crisis in the apparatus charged with bringing different classes into existence—in particular, that of the ruled in relation to the central power. With the slow disappearance of the working class, which has resulted from the weakening of the political parties and trade unions that once represented it, a vast field of communities with which to identify has been offered to individuals. The slow erosion of class consciousness has left the field open for the establishment of a palette of ethnic identities that anyone can choose from, based on paternal or maternal ancestors or on any other realm of social life. The emergence of what could be called "identities of consolation" can be understood in that way. These new identities, the result of a hardening of different communities, give individuals the illusion of being able to define themselves as they see fit. They also lead to a reassessment of the past, which is expressed as an intensification of the "duty to remember."[43]

The dispersal of social groups into communities is the most visible manifestation, if not of the weakening of the state, at least of the transformation of a nation-state possessing social classes into a communitarian state. In becoming communitarian, the state lets a play of mirrors come between itself and the communities. The spokespersons for the various communities—Jewish, Armenian, Muslim, and so on—thus claim a monopoly on representing the discrete set of individuals who, in one way or another, identify themselves as Jews, Armenians, or Muslims, and the state consents to give them credence as the only legitimate representatives.[44] By broadening customary law, the state produces communities, and these communities become more rigid in attempting to shift the power relations between religion and politics in their favor and in trying to introduce their own practices into the public realm, practices that, within the context of republican secularism, once belonged only to the private sphere.[45]

A Latent Communitarianism

Although assimilation has constantly been asserted as one of the pillars of the Republic, its application has always been a sensitive matter, as attested by the hesitancy the French state has demonstrated regarding the custom of circumcision. In fact, the process of establishing a sharp dividing line between the public and the private and of transforming the different "nations" or "communities" into religions is not always easy. As a constructed phenomenon, secularism is the result of a power relation and, as such, it can always be modified as a function of more or less explicit political imperatives.

The debates on regionalism in the 1970s and on multiculturalism in the 1980s attest to the difficulties of large portions of the French public to form a clear position on the matter. Although it seems logical that the political right and fundamentalist Catholic groups would wish to attack the state's secularism by "re-communitarianizing" the state, it may seem odder that a portion of the left, which has always defined itself by the watchword of secularism, should, on the pretext of defending collective identities, also wish to embark on a crusade against a secularism that creates a level playing field. It is undoubtedly within the context of a weakening in the processes of republican integration and the decline of the French empire that we need to situate the rise of regionalism in the 1970s and the trend toward multiculturalism in the 1980s.[46] Although the regionalist movement has recently lost steam and decentralization has managed to channel particularist demands, the nationalist movement in Corsica continues to struggle vigorously to obtain recognition of the island's cultural specificity and autonomy, or even its complete independence. That struggle has produced some results, since the state tried to give credence to that specificity by proposing the notion of the "Corsican people, a component of the French people." It was only through the vigilant attention of the Constitutional Council that that breach in the republican concept of nation was disallowed. Nevertheless, multiculturalism represents an expanding sector of the French legal system, though as yet it concerns primarily immigrant workers, especially from the Maghreb or sub-Saharan Africa.

The practice of ritual excision of the female genitals represents a privileged arena for defining the sphere of customary law. In the African colonies, the French administration, unlike the English, displayed leniency toward the custom; but ritual excision is now being repressed in France.[47] Jurisprudence, especially in the matter of excision, has tended recently to deal with offenders with increasing severity, and the legal definition of excision now treats the offense as a crime (and no longer as a misdemeanor). Penalties are increasing and on principle include prison time.[48] In 1991, at a trial at which anthropologists were called upon to testify, a woman who had come specially from Mali to perform the ritual procedure was sentenced to five years in prison. In the majority of cases, however, the accused are given suspended sentences. Thus, on 15 September 1994, the criminal court acquitted a woman from Mali and a Mauritanian man who had acknowledged subjecting their respective daughters to ritual excision. Another Malian woman, who was believed to have performed the procedure on children in a professional capacity, was given a suspended one-year sentence for "voluntary assault and battery on children under fifteen years resulting in mutilation."[49] These relatively lenient sentences, pronounced for acts dating back to 1984, betray the quandaries of a justice system confronted with a crime involving no criminal intent and where no specific law applies.[50] In the harshest sentence given, the justice system also recognized the force of custom exerted on the parents. As Dr. Michel Erlich, a psychiatrist and anthropologist specializing in sexual mutilation, declared during the trial, "the custom is absolutely obligatory. It is said that, if it is not done, the girl will be unable to marry. It is *the* rite of passage. Prior to it, one is not a woman." The recognition of the "rule of custom" on foreign populations demonstrates the existence of a gray zone in the French penal system or, more exactly, a zone outside the law reminiscent of "personal status" as it existed under the old colonial law.

In an area related to ritual excision, for about ten years, parallel rulings by the Conseil d'Etat (Montcho judgment of 11 July 1980) and the Cour de Cassation have opened the way in France to recognizing the validity of polygamous marriages by foreigners who have settled in the country after being married abroad. International agreements tending in the same direction have been concluded with certain countries of the Maghreb.[51] Finally, the Conseil d'Etat, in line with an opinion handed down in 1989, has shifted the power relations between religion and politics—between public and private—with the Kherouaa decision of 2 November 1992 ruling on the lawfulness of "Islamic headscarves." According to that decision, freedom of expression and legal access to education mean that "the wearing of signs by which students intend to display their adherence to religion is not itself incompatible with the principle of secularism," provided that the act does not constitute pressure, provocation, proselytism, or propaganda. The circular sent out by François Bayrou, minister of national education, moved in the opposite direction, in that it established a distinction between "ostentatious signs" that are "in themselves elements of proselytism" and "more discreet signs . . . that cannot raise the same objections." The "Islamic headscarves" were targeted, whereas Jewish yarmulkes and Christian crosses were exonerated of all suspicion of fundamentalism. Hence, through the latest incarnation of the "Islamic headscarf" affair, the old colonial Muslim policy, centered on the search for and promotion of a "moderate, tolerant, discreet Islam," is being pursued.[52]

The continuation of a nativist policy is even clearer in the case of the government's attitude toward the autochthonous peoples in the overseas territories, whose right of self-determination has been recognized. Under cover of new distinctions between populations enjoying a "local status" and those possessing a "common status," the old opposition between indigenous people governed by personal status and Europeans governed by the Civil Code has been continued. Similarly, the government has recognized the existence of ethnic groups as specific categories by constituting customary consultation councils in New Caledonia, thus giving credence to the idea of a Kanak culture common to the thirty-some tribes peopling the island.[53] In the same vein, former prime minister Edouard Balladur, during a meeting with the native Americans of Guiana, elaborated a notion of equality that is inconsistent with the orthodoxy of assimilationism and that provides a place within the Republic for each culture or tradition.[54]

The Conseil d'Etat, in refusing to endorse the notion of the "Corsican people, a component of the French people," asserted the atomization of French citizens in face of the omnipotence of the republican state. Nevertheless, during discussions accompanying that decision, the notion of the "French people" was reportedly accepted as the foundation of national identity.[55] It is true that any recognition of the legitimacy of autonomist claims to a parcel of national territory on the basis of the cultural specificity of the "autochthonous" populations, leads, through a ricochet effect, to the emergence of the notion of a "French people," just as the recognition of immigrant communities hardens or ethnicizes French identity as a counterreaction. There is thus currently a place for a true French multiculturalism, which is being deployed in the overseas departments and territories but which may also be realized in "metropolitan" France in connection with the rise of jus sanguinis.

The Rights of Peoples, the Rights of Man, and the Rights of the Individual

Faced with the new identity movements—that is, with the recomposition of ethnic groups or communities—republican secularism, founded on an atomistic conception of citizenship, is cracking everywhere. The republican posture, confronted with that proliferation of identities, that French-style political correctness, is now torn between a defense of the right of peoples and a defense of the rights of the individual. Every person has the right to embrace a chosen identity, and it is unclear on what basis that right could be denied. There is a limit, however, to the expression of cultural, ethnic, or religious particularism: anyone has the right to assume any identity he or she likes, as long as it does not threaten others; and it is at this point that we face once more the problem of the rights of man or, more precisely, of individual rights.

On a global scale, it is difficult to defend the rights of man as a single entity, since, in the Enlightenment tradition, the philosophy of the rights of man discredits the legitimacy of any public expression of ethnicity or religion on the pretext that they entail fanaticism, despotism, and ignorance. But religion is not simply ideology: it is also a system for making sense of the world. Ethnicity is not merely false consciousness: it is also a language that articulates the social.[56] At this stage of exacerbated identities, whether that identity is ethnic, nationalist, or fundamentalist religious, the issue is not to eradicate differences in the name of a secular fundamentalism, which would merely be the opposite and symmetrical form of the shortcomings it claims to denounce. It is the right and duty of those who defend an open republican position to show, when a particularist demand makes universal claims, how that identity, to borrow Franz Boas's expression, "has come to be what it is." In the case of France, the play of mirrors between the state, community spokespersons, and the far right, a play of mirrors that imprisons individuals in the stigma of an identity and constrains them to define themselves univocally, would thereby be shattered. In that case, by unveiling how identities are constructed, republicans would relativize the claims of social actors, in such a way as to arrive at a compromise between the interests of the individual and those of collectivities. In its role as defender of human rights, the republican attitude would consist of deconstructing identities to protect what is universal in each of us.

Notes

PREFACE

1. On this theme, see J.-L. Amselle, *Branchements, anthropologie de l'universalité des cultures* (Paris: Flammarion, 2001).
2. M. Foucault, *Il faut défendre la société* (Paris: Gallimard-Le Seuil, 1997). For a critical review of this book, see J.-L. Amselle, "Michel Foucault et la guerre des races," *Critique* 606 (1997): 787–800.
3. P. Bourdieu, *Méditations pascaliennes* (Paris: Le Seuil, 1997) [*Pascalian Meditations*, trans. R. Nice (Stanford: Stanford University Press, 2000)].
4. A. Touraine, *Pourrons-nous vivre ensemble? Egaux et différents* (Paris: Fayard, 1997).
5. I should note that there is also an individualist variant of liberalism.
6. On this subject, see G. Procacci, *Gouverner la misère, la question sociale en France, 1789–1848* (Paris: Le Seuil, 1993), 310, 311.
7. This point of view is particularly well represented in A. Minc's *L'ivresse démocratique* (Paris: Gallimard, 1995).
8. It is striking that the payment of family allocations and education grants under budget constraints, and even the progressive income tax, have been reconfigured in terms of the principle of so-called affirmative action or French-style equity. This suggests how deeply French government officials have been influenced by North American ideology. See the 1996 public report of the Conseil d'Etat, *Sur le principe d'égalité*, Studies and Documents no. 48 (Paris: La Documentation Française, 1997), 89. In fact, the French revolutionaries "already" had the idea of a progressive tax. See J.-P. Gross, "Le

liberalisme égalitaire des Jacobins," *Le Monde diplomatique,* September 1997.

9. "As one observes . . . in the United States, affirmative action can have the psychological consequence of publicly classifying one category of the population as in need of assistance and of stigmatizing them." Conseil d'Etat, *Sur le principe d'égalité,* 91.

10. On this subject, see the works of M. Tribalat and his team who, in a well-intentioned effort to show that the integration process continues to operate successfully, use the categories of "native French" and "ethnic groups," the same ones used by the National Front. M. Tribalat, *Faire France, une enquête sur les immigrés et leurs enfants* (Paris: La Découverte, 1995).

11. See J. Habermas and J. Rawls, *Débat sur la justice politique* (Paris: Cerf, 1997), 186.

12. On this subject, see H. Le Bras, *Le démon des origines, démographie et extrême droite* (La Tour d'Aigues: L'Auge, 1998).

13. On this theme, see Amselle, *Branchements.*

14. On the eminently fluid character of the notion of "gene," particularly in the identification of "hereditary illnesses," see A. Pichot, *Histoire de la notion de gène* (Paris: Flammarion, 1999).

INTRODUCTION

1. J.-L. Amselle, "L'anthropologue face au durcissement des identités," *Chimères* 26 (1995): 153–62.

2. L. Poliakov, *Le mythe aryen: Essai sur la source du racisme et des nationalismes* (Paris: Calmann-Lévy, 1971), 48. See also J. Barzun, *The French Race* (New York: Columbia University Press, 1932).

3. See especially M. Foucault, *Il faut défendre la société,* course at the Collège de France, 1976; M. Dietler, "Our Ancestors the Gauls," *American Anthropologist* 96, 3 (1994): 584–605, special issue on "Archeology, Ethnic Nationalism, and the Manipulation of Celtic Identity in Modern Europe"; and D. Franche, "Généalogie du génocide rwandais. Hutu et Tutsi: Gaulois et Francs," *Les Temps Modernes* 582 (May–June 1995): 1–58.

4. On the complementarity of Boulainvilliers's and Mably's ideas, see F. Furet and M. Ozouf, "Deux légitimations historiques de la société française: Mably et Boulainvilliers," *Annales: Economies, Sociétés, Civilisations* (henceforth *Annales ESC*) 34, 3 (May–June 1979): 438–50.

5. "Who were those Franks, and where did they come from, who in very small numbers and in very little time seized all of Gaul, which Caesar had taken ten years to subjugate? I have just read an author who begins with these words: 'The Franks, from whom we are descended . . .' Well, my friend, who told you that you are descended directly from a Frank? Hildvic or Clodvic, whom we call Clovis, probably had no more than twenty thousand poorly dressed and poorly armed men when he subjugated eight to ten million foreigners, Celts or Gauls, who were held in servitude by three or four Roman legions. We do not have a single house in France that can demonstrate the slightest probability, much less the slightest proof, that it had a Frank as its founder" (Voltaire, *Dictionnaire philosophique*, s.v. "Franc ou franq, France, François, Français").

6. E.-J. de Sieyès, *Qu'est-ce que le tiers état?* (1789), preface by J. Tulard (Paris: PUF, 1982), 32–33.

7. Karl Marx, letter to Joseph Weydemeyer, 5 March 1852.

8. Dietler, "Our Ancestors the Gauls." That schema of the war between the races, however, was able to reemerge in the twentieth century in Jean Jaurès's speeches and in the works of Charles Maurras and Maurice Barrès. See Barzun, *The French Race*, 258.

9. E. Conte and C. Essner, *La quête de la race, anthropologie du nazisme* (Paris: Hachette, 1995).

10. Is there any need to point out that this concept of mixing has nothing to do with the form I defend in *Logiques métisses: Anthropologie de l'identité en Afrique et ailleurs* (Paris: Payot, 1990) [*Mestizo Logics: Anthropology of Identity in Africa and Elsewhere*, trans. C. Royal (Stanford: Stanford University Press, 1998)]?

11. See the entire issue of *Esprit* devoted to this theme (June 1995).

12. On this subject, see J. McCumber, "Dialectial Identity in a Post-Critical Era: A Hegelian Reading," *South Atlantic Quarterly* 94, 4 (Fall 1995): 1145–60, special issue on "Nations, Identities, Cultures."

CHAPTER 1. THE HUMAN SCIENCES, NATURAL LAW, AND THE APPROACH TO DIFFERENCE

1. B. Barret-Kriegel establishes quite a clear contrast between an Anglo-Saxon tradition of natural law (Baruch Spinoza, John Locke, the U.S. Bill of Rights) and a French tradition (Jean-Jacques Rousseau, the Declaration of the Rights of Man and of the Citizen). See B. Bar-

ret-Kriegel, *Les droits de l'homme et le droit naturel* (Paris: PUF, 1989). Nevertheless, the Egyptian expedition was undertaken in the name of safeguarding the right to property, a natural right par excellence, and in the French colonies of sub-Saharan Africa only customs not contrary to "natural law" were preserved. See M. de Chabrol, "Essai sur les moeurs des habitants modernes de l'E-gypte," in *La description de l'Egypte*, 2d ed. (n.p.: Panckoucke, 1826), 18:272. See also Governor General Roume, quoted by Maupoil in *Coutumiers juridiques de l'Afrique-Occidentale française:* vol. 1, *Sénégal* (Paris: Larose, 1938), 4.

2. The structuralist Lévi-Strauss is that of *Les structures élémentaires de la parenté* (Paris: Mouton, 1967) [*The Elementary Structures of Kinship*, trans. James Harle Bell, John Richard von Sturmer, and Rodney Needham (Boston: Beacon Press, 1969)], the culturalist that of *Race et histoire* (1961; Paris: Denoël-Gonthier, 1984) [*Race and History* (Paris: UNESCO, 1968)].

3. In *Islands of History* (Chicago: University of Chicago Press, 1985), M. Sahlins adopts the two postures by turns.

4. L. Strauss, *Natural Right and History* (Chicago: University of Chicago Press, 1953), chaps. 3 and 4.

5. Ibid.

6. M. Villey, *Le droit et les droits de l'homme* (Paris: PUF, 1983).

7. A. Dufour, *Droits de l'homme, droit naturel et histoire* (Paris: PUF, 1991).

8. G. W. Leibniz, *Principes de la nature et de la grâce fondés en raison. Principes de la philosophie ou monadologie* (Paris: PUF, 1986).

9. Hugo Grotius, *De jure praedae commentarius* (1604).

10. Idem, *De jure belli ac Pacis* (1646).

11. P. Haggenmacher, *Grotius et la doctrine de la guerre juste* (Paris: PUF, 1983).

12. Hugo Grotius, *The Law of Peace and War* (Indianapolis: Bobbs-Merrill, 1962), 10–11, 38–41.

13. Samuel von Pufendorf, *De officio hominis et civis juxta legem naturalem libri duo*.

14. Ibid.

15. Ibid.

16. Ibid.

17. T. Hobbes, *Leviathan* (1651; London: Penguin, 1968), 188, 190.

18. "And thus much shall suffice; concerning what I find by speculation, and deduction, of Soveraign Rights, from the nature, need, and

designes of men, in erecting of Commonwealths, and putting themselves under Monarchs, or Assemblies, entrusted with power enough for their protection" (Hobbes, *Leviathan*, 257).

19. Sahlins essentially considers Hobbes's "state of nature" a fiction. See M. Sahlins, *Tribesmen* (Englewood Cliffs, N.J.: Prentice Hall, 1968), 7, n. 5.

20. "And in all places, where men have lived by small Families, to robbe and spoyle one another, has been a Trade, and so farre from being reputed against the Law of Nature, that the greater spoyles they gained, the greater was their honour, and men observed no other Lawes therein, but the Lawes of Honour; that is, to abstain from cruelty, leaving to men their lives, and instruments of husbandry. And as small Familyes did then; so now do Cities and Kingdomes which are but greater Families (for their own security) enlarge their Dominions, upon all pretences of danger, and fear of Invasion, or assistance that may be given to Invaders, endeavour as much as they can, to subdue, or weaken their neighbours, by open force, and secret arts, for want of other Caution, justly; and are remembred for it in after ages with honour" (Hobbes, *Leviathan*, 224).

21. Sahlins, *Tribesmen*, 4–9. I also use the Hobbesian model of war to account for the precolonial period in Wasolon. See Amselle, *Logiques métisses*, 212 [*Mestizo Logics*, 139].

22. M. Sahlins, *Stone Age Economics* (Chicago: Aldine-Atherton, 1972), chap. 4.

23. R. Filmer, *Patriarcha: On the Natural Power of Kings* (1680), in *Patriarcha and Other Political Works*, ed. P. Laslett (Oxford: Blackwell, 1949).

24. J. Locke, *An Essay Concerning the True Original, Extent, and End of Civil Government* (1690; New York: Gryphon, 1992), 242, emphasis in the original.

25. Ibid., 303–19.

26. H. Kuklick, *The Savage Within: The Social History of British Anthropology, 1885–1945* (Cambridge: Cambridge University Press, 1991), chap. 6.

27. Thomas de Zengotita, "The Functional Reduction of Kinship in the Social Thought of John Locke," in *Functionalism Historicized*, ed. G. W. Stocking (Madison: University of Wisconsin Press, 1984), 10–30.

28. Aristotle, *Politics*, 3.1: "The City and the Regime," trans. Carnes Lord (Chicago: University of Chicago Press, 1985). "As I see it, hu-

man social organization emerges as some kind of balance, stable or not, between the political order—Aristotle's *polis*—and the familial or domestic order—the *oikos*—a balance between polity and kinship" (M. Fortes, "An Anthropologist's Apprenticeship," in *Cambridge Anthropology* 8 [1983]: 30–31, special issue in memory of Meyer Fortes).

29. J.-J. Rousseau, *Discours sur l'origine de l'inégalité parmi les hommes* (1755; Paris: GF-Flammarion, 1971); idem, *Du contrat social* (1762; Paris: GF-Flammarion, 1966), 42.

30. On this point, see R. Derathé's fundamental *Jean-Jacques Rousseau et la science politique de son temps* (1950; Paris: Vrin, 1974), chap. 3.

31. Rousseau, *Discours sur l'inégalité*, 195.

32. Ibid., 209–11.

33. Ibid., 205ff.

34. Ibid., 211.

35. J.-J. Rousseau, *Du contral social*, 42.

36. Idem, *Discours sur l'inégalité*, 211, n. 1.

37. Sahlins, *Stone Age Economics*, 171.

38. C. Lévi-Strauss, *Tristes tropiques* (Paris: UGE, 1962), 282 [*Tristes Tropiques*, trans. J. Weightman and D. Weightman (New York: Penguin, 1992)].

39. Ibid., 351ff.

40. See J. Herder, *Ideen zur Philosophie der Geschichte des Menschheit* (1784).

41. Idem, *Auch eine Philosophie der Geschichte* (1774).

42. C. Lévi-Strauss, *Le regard éloigné* (Paris: Plon, 1983), 50 [*The View from Afar*, trans. J. Neugroschel and P. Hoss (Chicago: University of Chicago Press, 1992)].

43. E. Burke, *Reflections on the Revolution in France* (1790; Stanford: Stanford University Press, 2001).

44. A. Kuper, *The Invention of Primitive Society* (London: Routledge, 1988), 18.

45. Lévi-Strauss, *Le regard éloigné*, 50.

46. J. de Maistre, "Trois essais sur la France" (1794), in *Ecrits sur la Révolution* (Paris: PUF, 1989), 71–90.

47. Idem, *Considérations sur la France*, in ibid., 91–215.

48. Ibid., 145.

49. J. de Maistre, "Quatrième lettre d'un royaliste savoisien à ses compatriotes" (1793), in *Ecrits sur la Révolution*, 29–69.

50. Idem, *Démonstration philosophique du principe constitutif de la*

société. Méditations politiques tirées de l'Evangile (1830; Paris: Vrin reprint, 1985).

51. R. Nisbet, *The Sociological Tradition* (New York: Basic Books, 1966).

52. A. Thierry, *Récits des temps mérovingiens précédés de considérations sur l'histoire de France,* 2 vols. (Paris: Just Tessier, 1840).

53. Idem, *Histoire de la conquête de l'Angleterre par les Normands, de ses causes et de ses suites jusqu'à nos jours en Angleterre, en Ecosse, en Irlande et sur le continent* (1825; Paris: Furne, 1851).

54. J.-P. Chrétien, "Vocabulaire et concepts tirés de la féodalité occidentale et administration indirecte en Afrique orientale," in *Sciences de l'homme et conquête coloniale,* ed. D. Nordman and J.-P. Raison (Paris: Presses de l'ENS, 1980), 58; and Franche, "Généalogie du génocide rwandais."

55. Letter from Karl Marx to Joseph Weydemeyer, 5 March 1852. In that letter, Marx acknowledges his debt to Thierry and Guizot.

56. In this section, I follow Dufour's very complete *Droits de l'homme, droit naturel et histoire.*

57. On this subject, see Kuper, *The Invention of Primitive Society,* 22ff.

58. Ibid.

59. H. Maine, *Ancient Law* (1861; Boston: Beacon Press, 1963), 87ff.

60. Ibid., 118, 121, 165.

61. Ibid., 56, 139. For this section, I have referred to T. Metcalf's "Histoire, race et civilisation," lecture given at Lucette Valensi's seminar at the Ecole des Hautes Etudes en Sciences Sociales, May 1991.

62. G. W. Stocking Jr., *Victorian Anthropology* (London: Free Press, 1987), 124.

63. Kuper, *The Invention of Primitive Society,* 20.

64. De Zengotita, "The Functional Reduction of Kinship," n. 27.

65. T. Metcalf points out the tension in Maine's thinking between a liberal vision centered on the search for resemblance and a conservative vision anxious to foreground difference. See Metcalf, "Histoire, race et civilisation."

66. I am thinking in particular of D. Paulme, *Organisation sociale des Dogons,* ed. R. Maunier (Paris: Domat-Montchrestien, 1940). The book was published in the collection "Etudes de sociologie et d'ethnologie juridiques" (Studies of legal sociology and ethnology), and its editor was a professor and chair of colonial law at the Paris School of Law.

67. See R. Villamur and M. Delafosse, *Les coutumes agni rédigées*

d'après les documents officiels les plus récents (Paris: A. Challamel, 1901); M. Delafosse, *Haut-Sénégal-Niger* (Paris: E. Larose, 1912), vol. 1; *Coutumiers juridiques de l'Afrique-Occidentale française.*

68. On this subject, see Kuper, *The Invention of Primitive Society;* and Kuklick, *The Savage Within.*

69. Quoted in Kuper, *The Invention of Primitive Society,* 3.

70. A. R. Radcliffe-Brown, introduction to *African Systems of Kinship and Marriage,* ed. A. R. Radcliffe-Brown and D. Forde (London: Oxford University Press, 1950).

71. Ibid., 1. See also Lévi-Strauss, *Structures élémentaires de la parenté.*

72. See M. Fortes, "Time and Social Structure: An Ashanti Case Study," in *Social Structures,* ed. M. Fortes (Oxford: Clarendon Press, 1949). For a critique of Fortes's point of view, see T. C. Mac-Caskie, "State and Society, Marriage and Adultery: Some Considerations Towards a Social History of Pre-Colonial Asante," *Journal of African History* 22 (1981): 481, 492.

73. M. Fortes, "The Structure of Unilineal Descent Groups," *American Anthropologist* 55, 1 (1953): 17–41.

74. J. Barnes, "African Models in the New Guinea Highlands," *Man* 52 (1962): 5–9.

75. On this subject, see J.-L. Dongmo, *Le dynamisme bamiléké,* 2 vols. (Yaoundé: Centre d'édition et de production pour l'enseignement et la recherche, 1981).

76. C. Lévi-Strauss, "Réflexions sur l'atome de parenté," in *Anthropologie structurale II* (Paris: Plon, 1973), 103–35 [*Structural Anthropology,* trans. Claire Jacobson and Brooke Grundfest Schoepf (New York: Basic Books, 1963–75), 2 vols.].

77. E. Leach, *Rethinking Anthropology* (London: Athlone, 1961).

78. The notion of "jural system" is used by Needham. On this subject, see De Zengotita, "The Functional Reduction of Kinship," 28–29.

79. M. Verdon, *Contre la culture* (Paris: Editions des archives contemporaines, 1991), chap. 2.

80. Ibid.

81. P. Bourdieu, *Le sens pratique* (Paris: Editions de Minuit, 1980) [*The Logic of Practice,* trans. R. Nice (Stanford: Stanford University Press, 1990)].

82. E. P. Thompson, *The Making of the English Working Class* (New York: Pantheon, 1964).

83. E. Hobsbawm and T. Ranger, eds., *The Invention of Tradition* (Cambridge: Cambridge University Press, 1983).
84. J. Goody, *The Logic of Writing and the Organization of Society* (Cambridge: Cambridge University Press, 1986).
85. J. L. Comaroff and S. Roberts, *Rules and Processes* (Chicago: University of Chicago Press, 1981); M. Chanock, *Law, Custom and Social Order* (Cambridge: Cambridge University Press, 1986). A good overview of these points of view can be found in K. Mann and R. Roberts, eds., *Law in Colonial Africa* (Portsmouth, N.H.: Heinemann, 1991). See my review, "Le droit contextualisé," in *Cahiers d'Etudes Africaines* 124 (1991): 553–56.
86. S. F. Moore, *Social Facts and Fabrications: "Customary" Law on Kilimanjaro, 1880–1980* (Cambridge: Cambridge University Press, 1986).
87. See Amselle, *Logiques métisses.*
88. For a comparison with the Greek world, see G. Hoffmann, "Le 'Nomos,' tyran des hommes," *Droits et Cultures* 20 (1990): 19–30. For a continuist approach to the relation between vengeance and justice in Rome, see Y. Thomas, "Se venger au Forum. Solidarités familiales et procès criminel à Rome," in *La vengeance,* ed. R. Verdier and J. P. Poly (Paris: Cujas, 1984), 3: 65–100.
89. From this standpoint, the testimony of certain colonial administrators should perhaps not be rejected in toto. Let us consider what Aubert, commander of the Bougouni circle in 1932, says about Bambara customs: "Upon examination, custom turns out to be vague and shifting, variable from one canton to the next; and, most likely, justice was administered without fixed rules, by considering the persons in question and the circumstances. That does not mean that justice is capricious or lacking in equity: on the contrary, one has the impression that the natives have always had a very keen sense of equity." *Coutumiers juridiques de l'Afrique-Occidentale française:* vol. 2, *Soudan,* 8.
90. "Muslim law must not be systematically excluded from this list, on the pretext that it has sometimes undergone very profound alterations in contact with the traditional institutions of the animist environment that adopted it. It may nevertheless figure only in the last instance, since Koranic prescriptions currently constitute a sufficient foundation, in spite of the deforming influences of autochthonous jurisprudence" (Brévié, quoted by Maupoil, in *Coutumiers juridiques de l'Afrique-Occidentale française:* vol. 1,

Sénégal, 10). Oddly, Brévié, who grants only a marginal place to Muslim law, identifies the traces of Roman law in the populations of West Africa: "Those who have had the opportunity to study the Foulbé customs in the Niger delta, especially regarding paternal authority and matrimonial rule, have certainly been struck by the resemblance to Roman law" (ibid., 8).

91. "First under the influence of Islam, and spurred by the need to make cash transactions, marriage with the exchange of women is disappearing" (Aubert, in *Coutumiers juridiques de l'Afrique-Occidentale française:* vol. 2, *Soudan,* 71).

92. Patrilateral parallel cousin marriage is practiced by most Muslim groups in that culture area. See J.-L. Amselle, *Les négociants de la savane* (Paris: Anthropos, 1977).

CHAPTER 2. THE ORIGINS OF FRENCH MULTICULTURALISM

1. On this subject, see J. Frémeaux, *La France et l'islam depuis 1791* (Paris: PUF, 1991).

2. "Civilization will spread to the interior of Africa via Senaar, Abyssinia, Darfur, and Fezzan; several great nations are destined to enjoy the benefits of the arts, the sciences, and the religion of the true God, since it is through Egypt that the peoples of central Africa must receive enlightenment and happiness" (*Correspondance de Napoléon Ier. publiée par l'ordre de l'empereur Napoléon III,* vol. 29 of *Oeuvres de Napoléon Ier à Sainte-Hélène* (Paris: Imprimerie impériale, 1869), 514.

3. M. Ozouf, *L'homme régénéré. Essai sur la Révolution française* (Paris: Gallimard, 1989), especially 116–57. I draw liberally from this chapter of Ozouf's book.

4. Abbé Grégoire, *Essai sur la régénération physique, morale et politique des Juifs* (1788), preface by R. Badinter (Paris: Stock, 1988).

5. "To compare peoples, one must place them in the same circumstances; and what parity can be established between whites, enlightened by Christianity, which is more advanced than almost anything else, enriched by discoveries, surrounded by the teachings of every century, stimulated by every means of encouragement; and blacks, deprived of all advantages and destined for oppression and poverty? If not one of them had shown evidence of talent, there would be no reason to be surprised; what is truly astonishing is that

such a great number have manifested it. What would they be, there-fore, if, returned to their full dignity as free men, they occupied the place that nature assigned them and that tyranny denies them?" (Abbé Grégoire, *De la littérature des nègres ou recherches sur leurs facultés intellectuelles, leurs qualités morales et leur littérature* (1808), introduction by J. Lessay (Paris: Perrin, 1991), 280–81. On Grégoire's support of mixed unions, see ibid., 62–64; on develop-ment, see ibid., 282–83.

6. Nevertheless, for Volney, there was an essential difference between Europe and the East. In Europe, a fusion had occurred between the conquerors and the conquered and there was also a middle class. Nothing like that existed in Egypt and Syria, where the invaders re-mained totally distinct from the autochthonous peoples and there was no intermediate class. See Volney, *Voyage en Egypte et en Syrie* (1787), introduction by J. Gaulmier (Paris: Mouton, 1959), 114–15.

7. See H. Laurens, *Les origines intellectuelles de l'expédition d'E-gypte, l'orientalisme islamisant en France (1698–1798)* (Istanbul: Isis, 1987).

8. See Volney, *Les ruines, ou Méditation sur les révolutions des em-pires* (1791), ed. J. Tulard (Paris: Slatkine, 1979).

9. Volney, *Voyage en Egype et en Syrie*, 6, 10. On Volney's life and work as a whole, see J. Gaulmier, *L'idéologue Volney (1785–1820, 1951)* (Paris: Slatkine, 1980).

10. I have been greatly influenced on this point by Laurens's *Les orig-ines intellectuelles*.

11. "The sciences, long exiled, had to be brought back to the banks of the Nile." Fourier's preface to *Description de l'Egypte* 1: lxiv.

12. See H. Laurens, *Le royaume impossible, la France et la genèse du monde arabe* (Paris: Armand Colin, 1990), 13–18.

13. See E. Saïd, *Orientalism* (London: Routlege and Paul Kegan, 1978). For Saïd, the Orientalists invented the East by textualizing it. In fact, as J. Clifford has shown, it was actually Saïd who, in his cri-tique of Orientalism, reified the West, thus displaying a typically culturalist attitude. See J. Clifford, *The Predicament of Culture* (Cambridge: Harvard University Press, 1988), 21–54.

14. See Barret-Kriegel, *Les droits de l'homme et le droit naturel.*

15. "The right to property: a natural right that all lawmakers have held sacred and that only barbarians can disregard or violate. The tyrants of Egypt, in trampling every principle of wisdom and justice, did not respect that sacred privilege, which is both the foundation and

the guarantee of social happiness" (Chabrol, "Essai sur les moeurs des habitants modernes de l'Egypte," 18:242).

16. F. Gauthier, *Triomphe et mort du droit natural en révolution (1789–1795–1802)* (Paris: PUF, 1993).

17. Ibid., 185–87. Slavery was abolished in the colonies by the Convention of 4 February 1794; see ibid., 236.

18. See Laurens, *Les origines intellectuelles,* 74; Volney, *Les ruines,* 86.

19. Hence the sun lights the surfaces of the earthly globe cyclically, just as water flows downward, etc. See Volney, *Les ruines,* 253.

20. Ibid., 37–40.

21. Volney was a Voltairean. "Volney" was a nickname, formed by contracting "Voltaire" and "Ferney," the place where Voltaire was living, near Geneva.

22. Volney, *Les ruines,* 244–45.

23. Ibid., 105.

24. Volney, *Voyage en Egypte et en Syrie,* 59.

25. On Buffon, see K. Haoui, "Classifications linguistiques et anthropologiques de la Société d'anthropologie de Paris au XIXe siècle," *Cahiers d'Etudes Africaines* 129 (1993): 53. On the Copts' place within the black race, see Volney, *Voyage en Egypte et en Syrie,* 63–64; and idem, *Les ruines,* 176.

26. Volney, *Voyage en Egypte et en Syrie,* 64.

27. Ibid., 63–64.

28. Cheikh Anta Diop, *Nations nègres et culture* (Paris: Présence africaine, 1954); M. Bernal, *Black Athena, the Afro-Asiatic Roots of Classical Civilization,* vol. 1 (London: Free Association Books, 1987), and vol. 2 (1991). For a criticism of Bernal's ideas, see V. Y. Mudimbe, *The Idea of Africa* (Bloomington: Indiana University Press, 1994), chap. 3.

29. G. Boëtsch, *Egypte noire.* "The Copts, who are still Christians, are the former natives of the country. They number between ninety and a hundred thousand. They are not warriors; they are businessmen, collection agents, bankers, writers. They have their bishops, churches, and convents; they do not recognize the pope" (*Correspondance de Napoléon Ier* 29: 495).

30. For this entire section, I rely largely on *Correspondance de Napoléon Ier.* and on H. Laurens et al., *L'expédition d'Egypte (1798–1801)* (Paris: Armand Colin, 1989).

31. Quoted in Laurens, *L'expédition d'Egypte,* 75–77.

32. Laurens, *L'expédition d'Egypte,* 121.

33. Hence, to conform with the hygiene measures taken against the plague, residents of Cairo were obliged to spread out their clothing in the sun and to fumigate, which fomented discontent; L. Reybaud, *Histoire scientifique et militaire de l'expédition française en Egypte* (n.p.: A. J. Denain, 1830–86), 99, 139. To improve women's condition, Bonaparte had windmills built to liberate Egyptian women, who were toiling over hand-operated mills; see. R. Maunier, *Sociologie coloniale:* vol. 2, *Le progrès du droit* (Paris: Domat-Monchrestien, 1936), 92. "What would this fine country be after fifty years of prosperity and good government? The imagination delights in such an enchanting picture! A thousand locks would control the floodwaters and distribute them to every part of the territory; the eight to ten billion cubic units of water that are lost to the sea every year would be divided among all the lower parts of the desert . . . a great number of water pumps and windmills would lift the water into water towers, from which they would be drawn for irrigation; many waves of emigrants, arriving from remotest Africa, Arabia, Syria, Greece, France, Italy, Poland, and Germany, would quadruple its population; trade with India would resume along its ancient route through the irresistible force of the altitude; France, master of Egypt, would also be that of Hindustan" (*Correspondance de Napoléon Ier* 29: 513–14).

34. Laurens, *L'expédition en Egypte et en Syrie,* 288. See also Chabrol, "Essai sur les moeurs," 242–43: "There are no longer independent farmers on the banks of the Nile: mercenary laborers, or slaves crushed under the weight of the most odious vexations, reluctantly clear a few riverside lands, whose fruits they must not reap. . . . Hope no longer animates the laborer's zeal nor plucks up his courage, he now knows that a fierce stranger will collect the price of his sweat. . . . In that unfortunate region, the peasant is not a property owner and can never become one; he is not a farmer, he is born a serf of the faction oppressing his nation, he is the helot of the ancient Spartans, he is the unfortunate slave of the American colonists."

35. The expression "direct contact" refers to the policy conducted by W. Ponty in West Africa. See P. Marty, *La politique indigène du gouverneur général Ponty en Afrique-Occidentale française* (Paris: Ernest Leroux, 1915).

36. Reybaud, *Histoire scientifique* 2: 85.

37. The passage that follows is drawn from Reybaud, *Histoire scientifique.*

38. Chabrol, for example, insisted on the "need to base the legislative system on fixed and invariable foundations" ("Essai sur les moeurs," 241).

39. Throughout the French occupation, none of the fees connected to the investiture of judicial positions were collected. Ibid., 237–41.

40. Abd al-Rahman al-Jabarti, *Journal d'un notable du Caire* (Paris: Albin Michel, 1979), 250–64.

41. See Laurens, *L'expédition en Egypte et en Syrie*, 91–92.

42. In his proclamation of 4 Messidor, year VI, Bonaparte commanded his troops: "Respect the customs of the Muslims, as we respected the Italians and the Jews. Respect the muftis and the imams as we respected the rabbis and the bishops. The Roman legions protected all religions." Cited in Maunier, *Sociologie coloniale* 2: 202.

43. "Consulted on the important question of whether it was better to preserve the laws and customs governing property or to adopt Western laws, where property is incommutable and transmissible either by wills, or by donations from the living, or by freely agreed-upon sales, with the whole matter following established laws and forms, the great divan did not hesitate: it unanimously declared that Western laws were consistent with the spirit of the book of truth . . . and that the *feudal* principle [my emphasis] by virtue of which all land belonged to the sultan had been introduced by the Mongols, the Tartars, and the Turks, and that their ancestors had submitted to it only reluctantly" (*Correspondance de Napoléon Ier* 29: 592).

44. Letter from Poussielgue to the Directory (2–3 September 1799), in Reybaud, *Histoire scientifique* 4: 380–81.

45. Under Menou, "Estève, the administrator of finances, a zealous young man, eliminated many abuses and brought enlightenment to the tortuous administration of the Copts" (*Correspondance de Napoléon Ier* 30: 117).

46. "The fundamental principle of the Turks' and Mamluks' policy was to keep the sheikhs away from the administration of justice and government; they feared they would become too powerful. For these venerable old men, it was an agreeable surprise when they found themselves assigned the duties of civil and criminal justice, and even of all contentious affairs in the administration" (*Correspondance de Napoléon Ier* 29: 573–74).

47. Al-Jabarti, *Journal d'un notable du Caire*, 264.

48. Ibid., 233.

49. Reybaud, *Histoire scientifique* 3: 440–41.
50. Al-Jabarti, *Journal d'un notable du Caire*, 299.
51. Ibid., 166.
52. "In the opinion of the Arabs, whether farmers or Bedouins, the fellahs are their subjects; the Mamluks and the Turks are usurpers" (*Correspondance de Napoléon Ier*. 29: 469). [59] [rendering superscript]
53. Reybaud, *Histoire scientifique* 1: 114, chap. 4.
54. Ibid., 148–49.

CHAPTER 3. FRENCH MULTICULTURALISM IN ALGERIA

1. A. de Tocqueville, *De la colonie en Algérie*, ed. T. Todorov (Brussels: Complexe, 1988), 38.
2. Quoted by Laurens, *Le royaume impossible*, 56. See also the proclamation addressed to the Kouloughli (métis descended from Turkish men and Algerian women) by the French army: "We swear it by our blood: be united with us, be worthy of our protection, and you will reign in your country as you once did, independent masters of your native soil. The French will act with you as they acted thirty years ago with your *beloved brothers, the Egyptians*" (my emphasis). In H. Khodja, *Aperçu historique et statistique de la Régence d'Alger*, introduction by A. Djeghloul (Paris: Sinbad, 1985), 14.
3. M. Emerit, *Les Saint-Simoniens en Algérie* (Paris: Les Belles-Lettres, 1941), 53–56.
4. C.-A. Julien, *Histoire de l'Algérie contemporaine:* vol. 1, *Conquête et colonisation (1827–1871)* (Paris: PUF, 1979), 162. On Bory de Saint-Vincent and *Exploration scientifique de l'Algérie*, see also D. Nordman's forthcoming article, "Mission de savants et occupation: L'Exploration scientifique de l'Algérie (vers 1840–vers 1860)," 19 typed pages.
5. J. Frémeaux, *L'Afrique à l'ombre des épées*, thèse d'Etat, Montpellier, Université Paul Valéry-Montpellier III, 3: 607.
6. Bourmont's proposal for a capitulation agreement stipulated the surrender of the Casbah and the forts of Algiers and guaranteed the dey his freedom and the "possession of all his personal wealth"; it assured him of Bourmont's protection. The same was true for the militia. As far as the population was concerned, "the exercise of the Muhammadan religion will remain free; the freedom of all classes of inhabitants, of their religion, their property, their commerce,

their industry, will not be threatened; the women will be respected" (Julien, *Histoire de l'Algérie contemporaine*, 55).

7. On that contrast, see Laurens, *Le royaume impossible*, 58. I am indebted to L. Valensi for pointing out the segmentary nature of the precolonial Maghreb. See L. Valensi, *Le Maghreb avant la prise d'Alger* (Paris: Flammarion, 1969).

8. For this section, I rely primarily on Julien, *Histoire de l'Algérie contemporaine;* and Valensi, *Le Maghreb avant la prise d'Alger.*

9. Among the taxes, there was the Koranic tithe on harvests (*ashur*), the tax on cattle (*zakat*), the tax destined for maintaining the army (*lezma*), and the tax on non-Muslim lands (*kharadj*). See Julien, *Histoire de l'Algérie contemporaine,* 14.

10. As J. Dakhlia has shown, the institution of the *mehalla* cannot be limited to its taxing function. See "Dans la mouvance du prince: La symbolique du pouvoir itinérant au Maghreb," *Annales ESC* 43, 3 (May–June 1988): 735–60.

11. The qadi had very broad jurisdiction since he acted as judge, arbitrator, and notary. See Julien, *Histoire de l'Algérie contemporaine,* 5.

12. On the Muslim justice system in Algeria and the modifications introduced by the conquest, see A. Christelow's useful *Muslim Law Courts and the French Colonial State in Algeria* (Princeton: Princeton University Press, 1985).

13. Although the *kharadj* was abolished, all subjects continued to pay the *ashur,* the *zakat,* and the special taxes (*mauna*), in addition to fines. The collection of these different taxes was overseen by the agas. See Julien, *Histoire de l'Algérie contemporaine,* 184.

14. V. Monteil, "Les Bureaux arabes au Maghreb (1833–1961)," *Esprit* 300 (November 1961): 576.

15. Direct rule did not totally exclude the local headmen, but they were recruited by preference among the commoners, particularly from what are conventionally called the *makhzen.* See J. Frémeaux, *Les Bureaux arabes dans l'Algérie de la conquête* (Paris: Denoël, 1993), 95.

16. Thomas-Robert Bugeaud, "Circulaire du Gouverneur général à MM. les officiers généraux et colonels commandant les divisions, subdivisions et cercles, et à MM. les officiers chargés des affaires arabes, renfermant des instructions générales sur le gouvernement et l'administration des populations indigènes," in *Par l'épée et par la charrue,* writings and speeches by Bugeaud, ed. and intro. Gen-

eral Avan, foreword by C.-A. Julien (Paris: PUF, 1948), 182–83, my emphasis.

17. I. Urbain, "Du gouvernement des tribus," quoted in Emerit, *Les Saint-Simoniens en Algérie*, 236–37, my emphasis. In fact, Urbain is merely repeating the ideas of Pellissier de Reynaud, director of Arabic Affairs from 1837 to 1839 and author of *Annales algériennes* (1836–39). On this point, see X. Yacono, *Les Bureaux arabes et l'évolution des genres de vie indigènes dans l'ouest du Tell algérien* (Paris: Larose, 1953), 112.

18. On ethnic reductionism directed at the Arab and the Berbers, see A. Thomson, "La classification raciale de l'Afrique du Nord au XIXe siècle," *Cahier d'Etudes Africaines* 129 (1993): 19–36; F. Pouillon, "Simplification ethnique en Afrique du Nord: Maures, Arabes, Berbères (XVIIIe–XXe siècle)," *Cahiers d'Etudes Africaines* 129 (1993): 37–49; and, in general, this entire special issue of *Cahiers d'Etudes Africaines* ("Mesurer la différence: L'anthropologie physique").

19. For all matters relating to the Algerian policy of the Second Empire, see A. Rey-Goldzeiger, *Le royaume arabe* (Algiers: SNED, 1977).

20. Emerit, *Les Saint-Simoniens en Algérie*, 270–73.

21. The notion of "redemption" was one of the major themes of the English and U.S. abolitionists of the time, both whites and blacks. See F. Manchuelle, "Assimilés ou patriotes africains? Naissance du nationalisme culturel en Afrique francophone (1853–1931)," *Cahiers d'Etudes Africaines* 138–39 (1995): 333–68.

22. Rey-Goldzeiger, *Le royaume arabe*, 383.

23. For this account of the Arab Bureaux's areas of intervention, I have primarily consulted Yacono, *Les Bureaux arabes*; and Frémeaux, *La France et l'islam depuis 1791*.

24. The policy of cantonment corresponded to the Saint-Simonian or Fourierist doctrine of "association." "It is easy for the Arab Bureau to procure for our colons the native farmers they may need. The colons would like very much to follow that mode of operation, the only rational one at the start; and if these gentlemen will truly treat them with some humanity and not assault them at the first misunderstanding, this step made toward *association* [my emphasis] will unquestionably establish the first links in the chain that can connect the two peoples" (C. Richard, *Du gouvernement arabe et de l'institution qui doit l'exercer* [Algiers: Bastide, 1848], 68–69).

25. That idea was behind the "native providence societies."

26. E. L. Bertherand, *Médecine et hygiène des Arabes* (Paris: Germer Baillière, 1885), 553.

27. As Christelow has shown in *Muslim Law Courts and the French Colonial State* (136), the *medjles* or *majlis* was not a court of appeal prior to the conquest.

28. On that reform, see ibid.

29. An institution of Turkish origin. All the horsemen of a tribe or region were requisitioned for a limited time. See Frémeaux, *Les Bureaux arabes*, 87.

30. "Of all the scourges France must battle in Algeria, ignorance is indisputably the most terrible" (Captain E. de Neveu, *Les Khouan, ordres religieux en Algérie* [Paris: Guyot, 1846], 195).

31. Ibid. As G. Boëtsch and J.-N. Ferrié remark, the authors discussed by P. Lucas and J.-C. Vatin in *L'Algérie des anthropologues* (Paris: Maspero, 1975) were not anthropologists in the strict (French) sense of the term, that is, in the sense of physical anthropology. See G. Boëtsch and J.-N. Ferrié, "L'impossible objet de la raciologie, prologue à une anthropologie physique de l'Afrique du Nord," *Cahiers d'Etudes Africaines* 129 (1993): 5–18.

32. J. Berque, "Cent vingt-cinq ans de sociologie maghrébine," *Annales ESC* 11, 3 (January–March 1956): 296–324.

33. Frémeaux, *L'Afrique à l'ombre des épées*, 371.

34. A. Hanoteau and A. Letourneux, *La Kabylie et les coutumes kabyles* (Paris: Imprimerie nationale, 1873).

35. Durkheim's use of the works of Hanoteau and Letourneux and of Masqueray is too well known for me to dwell on it here.

36. It seems to me that this is the shortcoming of the special issue of *Cahiers d'Etudes Africaines* (129 [1993]) entitled "Mesurer la différence: L'anthropologie physique."

37. Frémeaux, *Les Bureaux arabes*, 26.

38. In the eighteenth century, the phenomenon of "degeneration" and hence of "regeneration" was linked to environment, and was associated with a monogenist attitude. See "De la dégénération des animaux," in G. Buffon, *Oeuvres philosophiques*, ed. J. Piveteau (Paris: PUF, 1954), 394–413.

39. See C. Blanckaert, "On the Origins of French Ethnology, William Edwards and the Doctrine of Race," in *Bones, Bodies, Behavior*, ed. G. W. Stocking (Madison: University of Wisconsin Press, 1988), 18–55.

40. Ibid., 42, n. 1.

41. Among the Berberophiles (Kabylophiles), Emerit lists Carette, Berbrugger, and Neveu, a group to which Bugeaud, Daumas, Hanoteau, Letourneux, and many others could be added. Conversely, Boissonnet, Lapasset, Lacroix, David, Urbain, Renou, and Jourdan were Arabophiles. See Emerit, *Les Saint-Simoniens en Algérie*, 250; and R. Germain, *La politique indigène de Bugeaud* (Paris: Larose, 1955), 213. Faidherbe was alternately an Arabophile and a Berberophile.

42. E. Pellissier de Reynaud, *Annales algériennes* (Paris: Anselin and Gaultier-Laguionie, 1836) 2: 441.

43. For an attitude favoring interbreeding, see E. L. Bertherand, *Médecine et hygiène des Arabes*, 555, n. 1, and, more generally, Dr. B. A. Morel, *Traité des dégénérescences physiques, intellectuelles et morales de l'espèce humaine et des causes qui produisent ces variétés maladives* (Paris: J.-B. Baillière, 1857). For the opposite view from the same era, see J. A. de Gobineau, *Essai sur l'inégalité des races humaines* (Paris: Firmin Didot, 1854).

44. Neveu, Urbain, Morelet, and Berbrugger married Muslim women; see Emerit, *Les Saints-Simoniens en Algérie*, 237. Pellissier de Reynaud went so far as to recommend polygamy; see Yacono, *Les Bureaux arabes*, 112. Richard recommended mixed marriages concluded on the basis of French or Muslim law, and for such cases "invented" the notion of Muslim French citizens: "We have French citizens who are Jewish, Protestant, and Catholic; why not add Muslim to that list?" (Yacono, *Les Bureaux arabes*, 113).

45. Emerit, *Les Saints-Simoniens en Algérie*, 47–53.

46. On Urbain, see F. Manchuelle, "Le rôle des Antillais dans l'apparition du nationalisme culturel en Afrique francophone," *Cahiers d'Etudes Africaines* 127 (1992): 375–408.

47. G. d'Eichtal therefore wanted to elevate the black woman through the infusion of white blood. Blanckaert, "On the Origins of French Ethnology," 43.

48. Julien, *Histoire de l'Algérie contemporaine*, 136.

49. See M. Daumas and M. Fabar, *La Grande Kabylie. Etudes historiques* (Paris: Hachette, 1847), 75–77.

50. See Hanoteau and Letourneux, *La Kabylie et les coutumes kabyles*.

51. According to the statute of 26 September 1842, the qadis continued to have jurisdiction among the Muslims only over all civil and commercial matters (art. 43) and all infractions committed by Muslims punishable by the law of the land in cases where, according to

French law, they did not constitute crimes or misdemeanors or in-fractions (art. 44). See Richard, *Du gouvernement arabe*, 71. On the 1854 reform, see Christelow, *Muslim Law Courts and the French Colonial State*.

52. "The government . . . wanted . . . to experiment in Algeria with the authority on which it might some day depend to regenerate, even in France, that part of the administration of justice" (M. P. de Mé-nerville, *Dictionnaire de la législation algérienne* [Paris: Philippe Conse, Durand, 1853], 378).

53. "Because the Arabs have no institution allowing them to impose the former [natural law], it is up to the supreme authority that governs them to fill the void" (Richard, *Du gouvernement arabe,* 47).

54. Ibid., 81.

55. "The jurists and magistrates, who speculate only about unified societies, have trouble recognizing that there can be justice in un-equal punishments for the same crime; but nothing is more equi-table in view of natural law, which dominates all other laws. Your task is to govern a people essentially different from our own" (ibid., 32). "The immediate application of our legislation to the Muslim people is thus materially impractical" (ibid., 79).

56. See Frémeaux, *L'Afrique à l'ombre des épées*, 411ff.; idem, *Les Bu-reaux arabes*, 238ff.

57. See Frémeaux, *L'Afrique à l'ombre des épées*, 411.

58. See Christelow, *Muslim Law Courts and the French Colonial State*, 136.

59. "Against those fanatical imposters who exploit the people's igno-rance, let us advance other Muslims cultivated by us, who will then be able to win their confidence and speak to them in the name of a common belief, but who will also inaugurate an era of peace and tranquillity among them" (E. de Neveu, *Les Khouan*, 194).

60. On the medersas, see Christelow, *Muslim Law Courts and the French Colonial State*, 145–48.

61. See Yacono, *Les Bureaux arabes*, 221.

62. See Berque, "Cent vingt-cinq ans de sociologie maghrébine."

63. Not all Arab Bureau officers were dupes to the belief in the impor-tance of trans-Saharan commerce. Regarding Tombouctou and the gold trade, E. Carette said: "The trade in *teber*, or gold powder, ac-counts in large part for its importance—a real importance, no doubt, but less so than what was long attributed to it by ignorance and credulity" (E. Carette, "Recherches sur la géographie et le com-

merce de l'Algérie méridionale," in *Exploration scientifique de l'Algérie pendant les années 1840, 1841, 1842:* vol. 2, *Sciences historiques et géographiques* [Paris: Imprimerie royale, 1846], 116.

64. On these two points, see Emerit, *Les Saints-Simoniens en Algérie,* 202–31; and Frémeaux, *Les Bureaux arabes,* 181–90.

65. In his appendix on the "most civilizable peoples of Algeria," Carette contrasts the peasants of the Tel—superstitious, fanatical, and lazy—to the nomads of the desert—watchful, hard-working, and enlightened—whom he calls "the Auvergnats of Algeria." In this passage, Carette develops his theory of "monitor" peoples: the French for Algerians in general, but also Saharans and Kabyles for the inhabitants of the Tel. See Carette, "Recherches sur la géographie," 235–41.

66. On the desire to thwart England and Morocco, see H. Duveyrier, *Exploration du Sahara. Les Touaregs du Nord* (Paris: Challamel, 1864), 293: "If the Touatians continue to try to close the Algerian route to French commodities and thus to unfairly advantage English commodities, it [the French government] will find itself obliged either to conquer Touat, which is not difficult, or to reopen the ancient route."

CHAPTER 4. FAIDHERBE

1. For the period immediately preceding Faidherbe's arrival in Senegal, see G. Hardy's helpful *La mise en valeur du Sénégal de 1817 à 1854* (Paris: Larose, 1921); and R. Pasquier, "Mauritanie et Sénégambie," *Histoire générale de l'Afrique noire:* vol. 2, *De 1800 à nos jours,* ed. H. Deschamps (Paris: PUF, 1971), 51–83.

2. On Roger's culturalism, see F. Manchuelle's helpful "Assimilés ou patriotes africains?"

3. See R. Pasquier's extremely valuable article, "L'influence de l'expérience algérienne sur la politique de la France au Sénégal (1842–1869)," in *Perspectives nouvelles sur le passé de l'Afrique noire et de Madagascar. Mélanges offerts à H. Deschamps* (Paris: Publications de la Sorbonne, 1974), 263–85.

4. For panegyrics, see the biographies of A. Demaison, *Faidherbe* (Paris: Plon, 1932); G. Hardy, *Faidherbe* (Paris: Editions de l'Encyclopédie française, 1947); and more recently, A. Coursier, *Faidherbe, du Sénégal à l'Armée du Nord* (Paris: Tallandier, 1989). In a

completely different direction, let me mention A. Bathily's dated article, "Aux origines de l'africanisme: Le rôle et l'oeuvre de Faidherbe dans la conquête du Sénégal," in *Le mal de voir* (Paris: UGE, 10–18, 1976), 77–107. See also L. C. Barrows's article in three parts, undoubtedly the most complete overview of the subject, but not free from bias: "L'oeuvre, la carrière du général Faidherbe et les débuts de l'Afrique noire française," *Le Mois en Afrique* 235–36 (August–September 1985): 120–50; 237–38 (October–November 1985): 130–56; and 239–40 (December 1985–January 1986): 120–50. See also idem, "Louis Léon César Faidherbe (1818–1899)," in *African Proconsuls*, ed. L. H. Gann and P. Duignan (New York: Free Press, 1978), 51–79.

5. See Barrows, "L'oeuvre, la carrière du général Faidherbe," part 1, 126–28.

6. See J. Frémeaux, *L'Afrique à l'ombre des épées*, 40.

7. See Barrows, "L'oeuvre, la carrière de général Faidherbe," part 1, 128–29.

8. "There is nothing in the world so dissimilar as Barbary and the Sudan, even though the geographers have delighted in joining them under the name 'Africa'" (Faidherbe, quoted in G. Hardy, *Faidherbe*, 149).

9. L. Faidherbe, "Lettre de M. Faidherbe à Monsieur le Président de la Commission centrale de la Société de géographie," 12 March 1853, in *Bulletin de la Société de Géographie de Paris* (February 1854), 129–30.

10. On this subject, see J. Schmitz's remarkable introduction to Shaykh Muusa Kamara, *Zuhur Al-Basatin* (forthcoming).

11. Think, for example, of the fate of the distinction between "warrior lineages" and "Maraboutic lineages," which continues to permeate the most recent anthropological writings. See L. Faidherbe, "Les Berbères et les Arabes du bord du Sénégal," *Bulletin de la Société de Géographie de Paris* (February 1854), 89–112.

12. Ibid.

13. Ibid.

14. Idem, *Le Zénaga des tribus sénégalaises. Contribution à l'étude de la langue berbère* (Lille: Danel, 1877), 95; see also idem, *Le Sénégal, la France dans l'Afrique occidentale* (Paris: Hachette, 1889), 16.

15. Faidherbe, "Les Berbères," 94.

16. Referring to the Maraboutic tribes who spoke Zenaga, Faidherbe de-

clared: "It would nevertheless be risky to conclude that the Berber element is much better than the Arab element. First, the mixing of two races, or even of three, if we include the black race, is almost universal in these populations; second, it was as a consequence of political events that the tribes of *tolba* became peaceful, and, though these Marabouts no longer commit violence themselves, they are only too often the instigators, especially against the infidels and when procuring slaves" (*Le Zénaga*, 91–92).

17. Idem, *Chapitre de géographie sur le nord-ouest de l'Afrique avec une carte de ces contrées à l'usage des écoles de la Sénégambie* (Saint-Louis, Senegal: Imprimerie du gouvernement, 1864), 9.

18. Idem, quoted in Barrows, "L'oeuvre, la carrière du général Faidherbe," part 1, 146.

19. Faidherbe devoted many studies to the Fulani. See especially L. Faidherbe, "Populations noires du bassin du Sénégal et du Haut-Niger," *Bulletin de la Société de Géographie de Paris* (May–June 1856), 281–300; idem, "L'avenir du Sahara et du Soudan," *Revue Maritime et Coloniale* (June 1863), 221–48; idem, *Essai sur la langue poul, grammaire et vocabulaire* (Paris: Maisonneuve, 1875); and idem, *Grammaire et vocabulaire de la langue poul* (Paris: Maisonneuve, 1882). On Faidherbe's writings on the Fulani, see H. G. Mukarovsky, "Contribution à l'histoire des langues peul, sérère et wolof," in *Itinérances en pays peul et ailleurs. Mélanges à la mémoire de P.-F. Lacroix* (Paris: Société des africanistes, 1988), 123–49; and A. Pondopoulo, "La construction de l'altérité ethnique peule et haalpulaar dans les écrits de Louis Léon César Faidherbe," *Cahiers d'Etudes Africaines* 143 (1996): 421–41.

20. In his later work, he relied on studies by M. Müller, who classified the different races as a function of their hair. See Faidherbe, *Essai sur la langue poul*, 11–12.

21. Idem, *Grammaire et vocabulaire de la langue poul*, 13.

22. Idem, "L'avenir du Sahara et du Soudan," 277.

23. As Mukarovsky notes in "Contribution à l'histoire des langues," 125.

24. The *métissage* between the Fulani and the blacks produced "more positive and practical ideas, a more subordinate spirit, greater muscular development, and love of the soil and agriculture" (L. Faidherbe, "Voyage de MM. Mage et Quintin dans l'intérieur de l'Afrique," in *Annales des voyages, de la géographie, de l'histoire et de l'archéologie* [Paris, 1866], 4: 10).

25. For a comparison between the history of Europe and that of Africa, see idem, *Notice sur la colonie du Sénégal et sur les pays qui sont en relation avec elle* (Paris: Arthus Bertrand, 1859), 62.

26. Idem, "Populations noires," 297.

27. Idem, "L'avenir du Sahara," 237.

28. "Similarly, there is a vast moral distance between them [the Bambaras] and those savage Negroes from the Guinea coast, who are still cannibals." The Bambaras were "far above those kings of Ashanti and of Dahomey who, even today, horrify the entire world with their cruel superstitions accompanied by human massacres" (idem, *Voyage de MM. Mage et Quintin*, 5–21).

29. See Barrows, "L'oeuvre, la carrière du général Faidherbe," part 2, 147.

30. Faidherbe, "Les Berbères et les Arabes," 90.

31. Barrows, "L'oeuvre, la carrière du général Faidherbe," part 2, 147.

32. "The major trade routes were hostile to the black race. [Faidherbe] preferred the crosscurrents from the sea, which brought a sense of well-being, justice, and peace, which would replace the darkness of ignorance and the grip of slavery" (Demaison, *Faidherbe*, 125–26).

33. Faidherbe, "Populations noires," 284.

34. Idem, *Voyage de MM. Mage et Quintin*, 113.

35. Idem, "Populations noires," 284.

36. "The members of the royal family, very proud of their race, are called Massassi. That family, in which a reddish-brown complexion, as opposed to the utterly black complexion of the inhabitants of the country, is considered a sign of nobility, claim to descend from white ancestors who came a very long time ago from very far away in the north, from Egypt, and were driven toward the Sudan by internecine wars, and especially, by the Arab invasion" (idem, *Les Dolmens d'Afrique* [Paris: Ernest Leroux, 1873], 416–17).

37. Idem, *Notice sur le Sénégal*, 29.

38. On Faidherbe's physical characteristics, see Barrows, "Louis Léon César Faidherbe," 52. On the theme of the blond warrior, see Gobineau, *Essai sur l'inégalité des races humaines*; and F. Nietzsche, *The Genealogy of Morals*, trans. W. Kaufmann and R. J. Hollingdale (New York: Vintage, 1967), 86–87.

39. Faidherbe, "L'avenir du Sahara," 245. Conversely, in North Africa, blacks had to intermarry with whites to adapt to the climate: "The two races [the Libyan and the Arab] manage well because they have

adapted to the climate, whereas the Negroes can survive there only thanks to interbreeding. The climate produces winters too cold for the former and summers too hot for the latter" (L. Faidherbe and Topinard, *Instructions pour l'anthropologie de l'Algérie, Considérations particulières par le général Faidherbe, Instructions particulières par le Dr Topinard* [Paris: Hennuyer, 1874], 11). On Faidherbe's raciology and his connections to Broca and Topinard, see the essays by K. Haoui and N. Coye in "Mesurer la différence: L'anthropologie physique," special issue of *Cahiers d'Etudes Africaines* 129 (1993).

40. According to Demaison, Faidherbe envisioned the creation of a "mixed race" possessing whites' faculties for organization and blacks' resistance to the oppressive climate. See Demaison, *Faidherbe*, 125.

41. On Faidherbe's hostility toward the métis traders, see L. C. Barrows, "The Merchants and Général Faidherbe, Aspects of French Expansion in Senegal in the 1850's," *Revue Française d'Histoire d'Outremer* 223 (1974): 236–83. On his defense and "practice" of *métissage* and his disputes with the Catholic Church, see Coursier, *Faidherbe*, 101–2. In 1857, Faidherbe had a son with a Senegalese woman. The boy was raised by Faidherbe's niece, who married in 1858. Faidherbe's son died of yellow fever in Saint-Louis at age twenty-four, while serving as a second lieutenant in the navy. Faidherbe also had an illegitimate daughter, who was taken in by the mother of an officer in the Saharan companies. See Frémeaux, *L'Afrique à l'ombre des épées*, 487.

42. "M. Faidherbe sometimes said that the only way to regenerate Senegal was marriage in the fashion of the country . . . [but] that he would not give his consent to an officer who requested his permission to be legally married to a local woman because it would dishonor a French family to introduce a woman of that kind into it" ("Lettre du supérieur général de la congrégation au ministre des Colonies, 15 août 1855," quoted in Coursier, *Faidherbe*, 102).

43. In adopting that view, Faidherbe joined a long republican tradition, as Hardy notes: "The period of revolutionary emancipation [in Senegal] coincided with the very paternal administration of 'good General Blanchot,' who had set an example of racial fusion by contracting a marriage in the fashion of the country" (Hardy, *La mise en valeur du Sénégal*, 10).

44. "It was especially by the native, and, to a lesser extent, by the métis,

naturally accustomed to the physical environment, that he expected Senegal to be developed" (Hardy, *Faidherbe*, 97).

45. "A great number of years ago, our ancestors, the first living beings, were merely little clumps of albumen without determinate form, growing through juxtaposition and multiplying by segmentation, as a result, without special organs" (Faidherbe, *Essai sur la langue poul*, 4–5). This passage can be compared to H. Spencer's *Principles of Sociology* (New York: D. Appleton, 1910).

46. Faidherbe, *Le Sénégal, la France*, 158.

47. That critical evaluation of the empire of El-Hadj Omar is also found among certain local actors. See Moustapha Kane, Sonja Fagerberg-Diallo, and David Robinson, "Une vision iconoclaste de la guerre sainte d'al-Haij Umar Taal," *Cahiers d'Etudes Africaines* 133–35 (1994): 385–417, special issue on "Archipel peul."

48. See Hardy, *Faidherbe*, 47; and Coursier, *Faidherbe*, 28. The same opinion is found in H. Azan, "Notice sur le Oualo (Sénégal)," *Revue Maritime et Coloniale* 19 (September–December 1863): 414–15. On the parasitic nature of the Wolof states according to Faidherbe, see M. Diouf, *Kajoor au XIXᵉ siècle, Pouvoir ceddo et conquête coloniale* (Paris: Karthala, 1990), part 3.

49. "The old African world, regenerated by Muslim semicivilization, galvanized by fanaticism, senses that it is through that breach of the Senegal Valley that the European race and its procession of ideas and institutions will before long penetrate the heart of that backward continent" (Faidherbe, *Voyage de MM. Mage et Quintin*, 15).

50. See Barrows, "L'oeuvre, la carrière du général Faidherbe," part 2, 144.

51. "Moreover, [Faidherbe] did not dream of attacking [Islam] so long as, for its part ... it ... confined itself to a purely religious realm" (Hardy, *Faidherbe*, 82). That sentence can be compared to the following passage by Richard: "We have French citizens who are Jewish, Protestant, and Catholic; why not add Muslim to that list?" (quoted by Yacono, *Les Bureaux arabes*, 113).

52. In terms of real property, for example, Faidherbe wanted to introduce private property and the registration of lands. See O. Leservoisier, "L'évolution foncière de la rive droite du Sénégal sous la colonisation (Mauritanie)," *Cahiers d'Etudes Africaines* 133–35 (1994): 73–74.

53. See Barrows, "The Merchants and Général Faidherbe."

54. On all these points, see Pasquier, "L'influence de l'expérience algérienne."

55. Ibid.
56. The commission, created in 1857, which included as members Brossard de Corbigny, Fulcrand, and Lize, met five times between 1867 and 1870. See P. Cultru, *Histoire du Sénégal du XVe siècle à 1870* (Paris: Larose, 1910), 370.
57. On Faidherbe's indirect rule, see W. B. Cohen's useful *Rulers of Empire: The French Colonial Service in Africa* (Stanford: Stanford University Press, 1971), 11ff.
58. See Hardy, *Faidherbe*, 52.
59. See Barrows, "Louis Léon César Faidherbe," 68–69.
60. On the situation in Algeria, see Richard, *Du gouvernement arabe*, p. 60, n. 1. In Senegal, the steam-powered mills were a failure; see Hardy, *Faidherbe*, 97.
61. Faidherbe, *Le Sénégal, la France*, 93.
62. Cultru, *Histoire du Sénégal*, 366–67.
63. Pasquier, "L'influence de l'expérience algérienne."
64. Ibid., 278.
65. "Because of the differences in race and religion, [Senegalese societies] must be allowed, as much as possible, to regulate their own affairs" (Hardy, *Faidherbe*, 78).
66. See Barrows, "Louis Léon César Faidherbe," 67.
67. See idem, "L'oeuvre, la carrière du général Faidherbe," part 2, 143. The "Arab" taxes (*ashur* and *zakat*) were introduced into Mauritania in 1904. See Leservoisier, "L'évolution foncière de la rive droite," 60.
68. See L. Faidherbe and Brosselard, *Le Soudan français, chemin de fer de Médine au Niger* (Lille: Danel, 1881–85), part 1, p. 18. "Let us return briefly to the question of Sudan and observe again that the greater part of that country, as fertile as India and well populated, does not have means of communicating with the rest of the world sufficient to impel it to produce and export its products in the interest of humanity as a whole, since these means are limited to a few caravans laboriously crossing the Sahara. Hence every Sudanese family confines itself to cultivating, in its own little garden, millet to feed itself and cotton and indigo to clothe itself" (ibid., part 2, p. 9).
69. "A single goal is to be achieved: new outlets that could spur the natives to higher production, by which means products of our French industries could spread to the dark continent" (Demaison, *Faidherbe*, 125).
70. He therefore expressed keen reservations about the Magnan proj-

ect, which consisted of sending steamboats up the Niger from its mouth in Bamako and of launching two caravans, one between Bamako and Bakel, the other between Tombouctou and Algeria. See Faidherbe, "L'avenir du Sahara et du Soudan," 247–48. On the Magnan project, see Emerit, *Les Saint-Simoniens en Algérie,* 225–29.

71. See Barrows, "L'oeuvre, la carrière du général Faidherbe," part 3, p. 132.

72. See ibid., part 2, p. 151.

73. Ibid.

74. See Barrows, "L'oeuvre, la carrière du général Faidherbe," part 3, pp. 121–32; Faidherbe and Brosselard, *Le Soudan français,* part 1, p. 13.

75. Jauréguiberry was governor of Senegal from 1861 to 1863, between Faidherbe's two terms. His policy was more centered on direct administration than was that of his predecessor. See Barrows, "L'oeuvre, la carrière du général Faidherbe," part 3, pp. 131–32.

76. On the conquest of the Sudan, see A. S. Kanya-Forstner, *The Conquest of the Western Sudan* (Cambridge: Cambridge University Press, 1969); and J. Méniaud, *Les pionniers du Soudan,* 2 vols. (Paris: Société des publications modernes, 1931).

77. According to R. Delavignette and C.-A. Julien, Roume (governor of French West Africa) wrote in 1929: "West Africa is a rational creation of the French mind, composed essentially of order and clarity. It proceeds, in fact, from the simple and very great notion of a man who must be considered its true founder, Faidherbe" (R. Delavignette and C.-A. Julien, *Les constructeurs de la France d'outre-mer* [Paris: Corrêa, 1946], 28–29).

78. See H. Brunschwig, "Louis-Gustave Binger (1856–1936)," in *African Proconsuls,* ed. Gann and Duignan, 110–11.

79. L.-G. Binger, *Du Niger au golfe de Guinée par le pays de Kong et le Mossi,* 2 vols. (Paris: Hachette, 1892). Some passages in this book are quite simply copied from Faidherbe's writings. Compare ibid., 1: 130–31, and Faidherbe and Bosselard, *Le Soudan français,* part 2, 8–9.

80. L.-G. Binger, *Esclavage, islamisme et christianisme* (Paris, 1891); idem, *Le péril de l'islam* (Paris, 1906). On this point, see Brunschwig, "Louis-Gustave Binger," 113. The idea that the inferior intellectual capacity of blacks could be attributed to the smaller size of their brains, an idea put forward by Binger, was taken directly from Faidherbe.

81. See H. Deschamps, *Gallieni pacificateur* (Paris: PUF, 1949), 17.
82. Ibid.
83. See Kanya-Forstner, *The Conquest of the Western Sudan*, 102.
84. See Barrows, "L'oeuvre, la carrière du général Faidherbe," part 3, 150; Manchuelle, "Assimilés ou patriotes?"; A. L. Conklin, *A Mission to Civilize: The Republican Idea of Empire in France and West Africa, 1895–1930* (Stanford: Stanford University Press, 1997).
85. "But [Faidherbe's] stroke of genius was not that he applied, with European logic, a well-conceived plan for the colonization of Senegal. On the contrary, it was that he grasped that Senegal was a colony of a very new kind, absolutely different from the West Indies and Réunion or from Algeria, which were the chief models of the time; it was that he observed Senegal not only in its local realities and sensibilities but in its relations to the dark continent as a whole; it was, finally, that he modified his plans in accordance with the empirical data he collected" (Delavignette and Julien, *Les constructeurs de la France*, 237).
86. On this subject, see J. V. Magistro, "Crossing over Ethnicity and Transboundary Conflict in the Senegal River Valley," *Cahier d'Etudes Africaines* 130 (1993): 201–32; J. Schmitz, "Anthropologie des conflits fonciers et hydropolitique du fleuve Sénégal (1975–1991)," *Cahiers Orstom, Sciences Humaines* 29, 4 (1993): 591–623; "Cités noires: Les républiques villageoises du Fuuta Tooro (vallée du fleuve Sénégal)," *Cahiers d'Etudes Africaines* 133–35 (1994): 419–60; and especially J. Webb, *The Desert Frontier, Ecological and Economic Change along the Western Sahel, 1600–1850* (Madison: University of Wisconsin Press, 1995).

CHAPTER 5. MULTICULTURALISM IN FRANCE

1. On the general problem of transforming "peasants" into "Frenchmen" and the secularization of France, see E. Weber, *Peasants into Frenchmen: The Modernization of Rural France, 1870–1914* (Stanford: Stanford University Press, 1976). For Weber, the France of 1870 can be assimilated to a colonial empire.
2. For all issues relating to the Jews before, during, and after the French Revolution, see S. Schwarzfuchs, *Du juif à l'israélite, histoire d'une mutation (1770–1870)* (Paris: Fayard, 1989).
3. For an African example, see J.-L. Amselle, "L'ethnicité comme

volonté et comme représentation, propos des Peuls du Wasolon," *Annales ESC* 2 (1987): 465–89.

4. Abbé Grégoire, *Essai sur la régénération.*
5. Ibid., 144–45.
6. Ibid., 144.
7. Ibid., 120.
8. Quoted by N. Rouland, *La tradition juridique française et la diversité culturelle,* report to the Commission Française pour l'Unesco (1993).
9. Ibid.
10. Schwarzfuchs, *Du juif à l'israélite,* 152.
11. Ibid.
12. Ibid., 171.
13. Ibid., 187ff.
14. Ibid., 222.
15. Previously, what had mattered for the Jews were the Hebrew given names of father and son. In the religious sphere, the family name was considered nothing but a nickname. Jews preferred to be known, and to sign their names, as "X son of Y." Hence the family name was not fixed, and sometimes the father bore a different family name from his son. See ibid., 215, 218–19.
16. Ibid., 323–27.
17. G. Mauco, *Les étrangers en France* (Paris: Armand Colin, 1932), 14.
18. Ibid., 8–14.
19. Ibid., 37.
20. See G. Noiriel, *Le creuset français* (Paris: Le Seuil, 1988), 71ff.
21. Ibid.
22. See Mauco, *Les étrangers en France,* 143.
23. On the Polish immigration during the interwar period and for a comparison with Italian immigration, see J. Ponty's very complete *Polonais méconnus, histoire des travailleurs immigrés en France dans l'entre-deux-guerres* (Paris: Publications de la Sorbonne, 1988).
24. Ibid., 156.
25. Ibid., 210, 384.
26. "These numbers show that the rate of naturalization, which had tripled since the war, was particularly rapid among immigrants from the neighboring countries, who were easily assimilated. It slowed considerably among those who came from farther away and were more different in every respect, whose fusion came about

more slowly and whose arrival was, in fact, more recent. That was the case for the Poles, who, proportionately, accounted for four times fewer naturalized citizens than the Italians and the Belgians" (Mauco, *Les étrangers en France*, 550–51). The culturalist explanation was—and still is—often the result of forgetting the history of the group considered. Under the Vichy regime, Mauco contributed to the review *L'Ethnie Française* (The French ethnic group), whose director was G. Montandon. See also the interesting position of R. Martial who, after defending the creation of Muslim centers in the name of cultural relativism, became an adversary of immigration because he considered the "interracial graft" impossible. On all these points, see W. H. Schneider, *Quality and Quantity: The Quest for Biological Regeneration in Twentieth-Century France* (Cambridge: Cambridge University Press, 1990).

27. "That mob of immigrants, some of them uprooted and poorly adapted, has led to an increase by one-third in the crime rate in France, and thus has indisputably had a demoralizing and destabilizing influence. No less pernicious is the moral decay of certain Levantines, Armenians, Greeks, Jews, and other 'wog' merchants and traffickers. The intellectual influence of foreigners, though difficult to discern, appears above all opposed to reason, delicacy, prudence, and moderation, traits that characterize the Frenchman" (Mauco, *Les étrangers en France*, 558).

28. M. Hovanessian, *Le lien communautaire, trois générations d'Arméniens* (Paris: A. Colin, 1992), 29.

29. For all questions concerning the Armenians, I make liberal use of Hovanessian's *Le lien communautaire*.

30. Ibid., 297.

31. See the analyses of D. Schnapper, *La France de l'intégration* (Paris: Gallimard, 1991).

32. See P. Weil, *La France et ses étrangers* (Paris: Calmann-Lévy, 1991), 55–65.

33. Especially *Mosaïque*, on channel FR3.

34. On this subject, see H. Tincq's articles in *Le Monde* "Séminaire pour imams," 3–4 October 1993; and "L'islam de France sur la voie de l'émancipation," 13–14 February 1994.

35. Note that the very idea of a "Church" is alien to Islam. That religion is not centralized and has no clergy.

36. See G. Kepel, *Les banlieues de l'islam* (Paris: Le Seuil, 1987), 65.

37. Quoted in Kepel, *Les banlieues de l'islam*, 71–72. On Lyautey's

Muslim policy, which is beyond the scope of this book, see D. Rivet, *Lyautey et l'institution du protectorat français au Maroc (1912–1925)* (Paris: L'Harmattan, 1988), vol. 2, chap. 17.

38. For all matters relating to the Soninke in France, I rely on M. Timera's remarkable *Les immigrants sooninke dans la ville: Situations migratoires et stratégies identitaires dans l'espace résidentiel et professionnel,* thesis for the Ecole des Hautes Etudes en Sciences Sociales, 1993 (forthcoming from Karthala). On African migration networks, see J.-L. Amselle, ed., *Les migrations africaines* (Paris: Maspero, 1976). See also C. Quiminal, *Gens d'ici, gens d'ailleurs* (Paris: Christian Bourgois, 1991).

39. On the "egalitarian" nature of Mali Wahhabism, see J.-L. Amselle, "A Case of Fundamentalism in West Africa: Wahabism in Bamako," in *Studies in Religious Fundamentalism,* ed. L. Caplan (London: Macmillan, 1987), 79–94.

40. This last aspect, inherited from Renan ("The nation is a daily plebiscite") emphasizes voluntary adhesion as a requirement for belonging to the French nation, in particular for the children of foreigners born in France.

41. Regarding the *harkis* in particular.

42. On this subject, see J.-L. Amselle, "Quelques réflexions sur la question des identités collectives en France aujourd'hui," in *Ethnicisation des rapports sociaux, racismes, nationalismes, ethnicismes et culturalismes,* ed. M. Fourier and G. Vermes (Paris: L'Harmattan, ENS Fontenay/Saint-Cloud, 1994), 44–54.

43. The reopening of the debate surrounding Vichy France and the revival of memories of the Jewish deportation, as they appear in the special section of the newspaper *Le Monde,* where, every day, the descendants of deportees commemorate the disappearance of their relatives, are particularly revealing in this respect.

44. Hence M. Siruk, chief rabbi of France, regularly discussed the options of open secularism versus closed secularism with F. Mitterrand. See H. Tincq, "La bataille du grand rabbinat," *Le Monde,* 16 June 1994.

45. On this subject, see in particular the controversy surrounding election day on Passover, 27 April 1994, during the second round of the cantonal elections. In *Tribune Juive* (10 March 1994), the chief rabbi of France warned the Jews not to go to the polls on a religious holiday, thus producing a polemic among the different authorities of French Judaism. See Tincq, "La bataille du grand rabbinat."

46. B. Jewsiewicki, "Le primitivisme, le post-colonialisme, les antiquités nègres et la question nationale," *Cahiers d'Etudes Africaines* 121–22 (1991): 191–213, special issue on "La malédiction."
47. On this subject, see *Droits et Cultures* 20 (1990), devoted to ritual excision.
48. Currently, French positive law relating to childhood sexual mutilation is defined by article 312 of the penal code, which bars assault and battery on minors under fifteen and prescribes criminal penalties. The old law stipulated misdemeanor penalties only. But the penal code targets criminals and not those acting under the rule of custom.
49. M. Peyrot, "Deux parents africains acquittés dans un procès d'excision," *Le Monde*, 17 September 1994.
50. Conversely, in Sweden, the United Kingdom, and Switzerland, the law clearly bans excision as such, but cases are not prosecuted. These three countries have decided to favor prevention through information. On this point, see J.-L. Amselle, "Le droit contextualisé," *Cahiers d'Etudes Africaines* 124 (1991): 553–56.
51. See Rouland, *La tradition juridique français.*
52. Speech by C. Pasqua, former minister of the interior, given on 30 September 1994 at the inauguration of the Lyons mosque.
53. In fact, these tribes all speak different languages. On this point, see A. Bensa, "Le centre culturel Jean-Marie Djibaou," *Journal des Anthropologues* 53–55 (1994): 155–60.
54. "The notion of equality has too often been taken in an overly legal sense. Everyone today is well aware that the notion of equality is not necessarily that of identity. . . . It is first and foremost respect for the dignity of others, for the traditions of others." According to the prime minister, there is no "contradiction" between "respect for each person's culture" and "solidarity within the Republic"; rather, the two traditions ought to coexist. See F. Bobin, "M. Balladur promet aux Amérindiens de Guyane le respect de leurs traditions," *Le Monde*, 24 May 1994.
55. Rouland, *La tradition juridique française.*
56. On the structuring (and not solely ideological) aspect of religion, see E. Escoubas's preface to the French edition of T. Adorno's *Jargon de l'authenticité* (Paris: Payot, 1989), 23–25; and M. Augé, ed., *La construction du monde* (Paris: Maspero, 1974).

Index